MAT PEMBER AND FABIAN CAPOMOLLA

THE LiTTLe VEGGiE PATCH Co

1-MINUTE GARDENER

plum   Pan Macmillan Australia

CONTENTS

Introduction 6

READY, SET, PREP!

Choosing the right spot for your patch 12

Choosing the right pot 14

Chasing the sun 16

Lining a recycled crate 18

Testing your soil for contaminates 22

Pimp your soil 24

How much compost do you need? 26

Getting the pH level right 28

Topping up a no-dig garden 30

Easy-peasy trellising 32

GET PLANTING

What time of year to plant? 36

What time of day to plant? 38

How to soak hard-coated seeds 40

How to plant seeds 42

How to plant seedlings 48

Easy incubator 52

Spacing your plants 54

Companion planting no-brainers 58

How to plant garlic 60

It's … tomato time! 62

Crop rotation no-brainers 64

PATCH (AND POT) LOVE

The best time to water your patch 68

Too much or not enough? 70

Picking seed heads 72

Culling seedlings 74

Why fan-spray watering is best 78

How to fertilise in pots 80

How to mulch 82

Pruning fruit trees 86

The art of pinching 90

Staking tomatoes like a pro 92

Hand-pollination for beginners 94

Pruning raspberries 98

Transplanting strawberry runners 100

THE LiTTLe
VEGGiE
PATCH CO

1-MINUTE

GARDENER

To my Mum and Dad,
for everything.

Mat

To Monty Don,
for inspiring a
career change.

Fabian

SHOO, PEST!

Zapping snails with copper tape 104

Netting made easy 106

Blossom end rot? Don't panic! 110

Stink-bombing possums 112

Caterpillars begone! 116

Coffee-spray your snails away 118

Keep it clean 120

What is a soapy spray? 122

Trapping snails with beer 124

GET PICKING

How to harvest herbs 128

Picking early-season tomatoes 132

Harvesting leafy greens 134

Pick more, grow more 138

How to harvest spring onions 140

The lowdown on edible flowers 142

When to pick your beetroot 144

Root refrigerator 148

AFTER THE HARVEST

Drying herbs 152

Making compost like dough 154

How to prune a chilli plant 156

Quick guide to trench-composting 158

Pickling vegetables 162

Fermenting waste systems 166

What worms really love 168

LITTLE HELPERS

Making dummy butterflies 172

Making egg-carton planters 176

Seed-bombing 178

Competitive snail-hunting 182

Decorating the patch 184

TOP 5

EASY-GROWERS 20

SHADE-LOVERS 46

CLIMBERS 56

SMALL-SPACE PLANTS 76

EDIBLE FLOWERS 114

INVINCIBLES 136

TOMATO VARIETIES 146

LEAFY GREENS 160

FAST-GROWERS 174

Acknowledgements 186

Index 188

When it comes to learning, there are basically two types of people: *book-smart* and *street-smart*. *Book-smart* types generally excelled at school, got the best marks and, eventually, the most high-paying jobs. *Street-smart* types generally excelled outside of school, got mediocre marks and ended up in more interesting jobs. One group of earners understood algebra, the other were better at catching public transport.

When we were at school it was pretty much a one-size-fits-all approach. We were all thrown into the same pot to learn mathematics, science and languages, with little concern about individual learning styles.

Not surprisingly, we picked up some bad habits. Rather than learning and understanding concepts, we learnt more how to memorise whole textbooks by writing and then rewriting them again and again. It was a form of study perfectly suited to the early years of late-night coffee-drinking and listening to emotionally tortured grunge music. Come exam time our minds could recollect information – like turning to a page marked in a book – and flood the paper with perfectly crafted, pseudo-plagiarised text. While in class we mostly pretended to listen and also learnt how to avoid answering questions. Head down, writing and nodding when we felt the heat, no teacher dared disturb a student in the depths of learning!

Of course, there were some great teachers – those who spent less time explaining the theory and more time showing it. They related abstract ideas back to our lives and found a way to make them resonate. Mr Yim was particularly memorable – a mathematics teacher who mixed algebra with tai chi. Maths suddenly became pretty cool, a lot more spiritual, and we understood … sort of. That Mr Yim was a good egg.

Gardening tends to attract a lot of passionate people who have a lot of really good things to say. Generally, though, gardening instruction is plagued by too much text rather than explanation of the practices, with too few examples actually *showing* them in action. The *book-smart* style of teaching and learning just doesn't suit something so inherently visual and practical.

Now that we are among those doing the teaching, we find inspiration every time we are able to show someone something completely new. Like the idea that all lettuce should be picked leaf by leaf, or to get the best out of spring onion cut it down to the base, or to grow garlic simply break a head apart and plant clove by clove. You can't imagine the number of people who think that to get one head of garlic you plant one head of garlic and then wait nine months. Okay, we would probably not entrust these people with our investment portfolios, but we won't hold it against them either. Many things are only obvious in hindsight and there will come a time in all of our lives when we have a garlic moment. At the very least, however, this book will help you avoid some gardening faux pas.

We know that when starting out you want to get things right; more importantly, you need to get things right to keep you interested. No matter how simple or complicated a task in the garden is, it always helps when someone leads the way and shows you how to do it first. It is then easier to take that experience and convert it into knowledge. For us, the best form of learning is seeing things being done.

Well before any formal schooling, there were years of informal lessons in the garden with our grandparents – people who didn't have much opportunity for education and so had no bias towards certain ways of learning. They learnt through example and they taught us through example, and a lot of time was spent looking at the veggie patch through their eyes.

Often we would just trail behind them, hanging onto a leg, getting a good look at whatever it was they were doing. That's when they slowed everything down for us – tying a tomato plant to its stake, mixing the chook poo through the sandy soil, even pulling out a weed was done in slow motion so methodically that it was permanently imprinted on us.

Those moments have stuck with us more than any lesson taught in a classroom. Who would have thought that an education lasting more than a decade barely taught us the chemical composition of magnesium and yet watching our Nonnos and Nonnas in the veggie patch would be so thorough and enlightening. Ironically, the first time we planted seedlings again in our adult lives – after a long sojourn – we stood back and watched someone else plant the patch out. Not for fear of failure or lack of knowledge, it was just comforting to watch and relearn.

By buying this book we assume you are already interested in growing food and we are not sitting in a classroom staring at each other, wondering how to push each others' buttons. (There is also the chance someone bought this book for you, perhaps to give you a hint. Good on 'em – they obviously know what is best for you.) We're sure you have plenty of questions and hopefully this book will help you answer them, even those that may seem too embarrassing to ask! It will certainly make you a better, faster grower of your own food. So what are you waiting for? Or it may be you're curious about the things Nonno and Nonna couldn't explain, only show, and we want to share those things with you too – clearly laid out, step by step.

In essence, we are team-sport people – we like the atmosphere and celebration of the team. Hopping into the garden and picking incredible produce all by your onesome is kind of like laughing at a joke by yourself – it is okay, but could be better – so we want to pull more people into the *great* adventure that is to be found all the way along the food trail.

Whatever competency you think you have in the garden, we invite you to come along and share it with us. While finding a better way to teach and learn is part of the picture, ultimately we want an edible gardening team that is better able to enjoy growing produce while laughing at crap jokes. We look forward to you joining us and would love to hear from you, so drop us a line at:

facebook.com/littleveggiepatchco
littleveggiepatchco.com.au
instagram.com/littleveggiepatchco

Fab and Mat

ONE
MINUTE
SKILLS

Choosing the right spot for your patch **12**

Choosing the right pot **14**

Chasing the sun **16**

Lining a recycled crate **18**

Testing your soil for contaminates **22**

Pimp your soil **24**

How much compost do you need? **26**

Getting the pH level right **28**

Topping up a no-dig garden **30**

Easy-peasy trellising **32**

TOP five ⟶ EASY-GROWERS **20**

READY,
SET,
PREP!

ONE
MINUTE
SKILLS

CHOOSING THE RIGHT SPOT FOR YOUR PATCH

Life was never meant to be easy, particularly when it comes to making important choices

And a few really key decisions aside – choosing your life partner, buying your house and deciding on the type of smart phone to use – picking the spot to put your veggie patch is pivotal. For that reason it is worth considering all mitigating factors.

Your veggie patch provides food and ensures you don't go hungry. Getting its position wrong could potentially alter the Earth's rotation. With Earth out of whack and vegetables not growing to their full potential, chaos would surely ensue and so the decision-making process needs to be well structured and composed.

In case you struggle with well-balanced, thoughtful decision making, we have neatly laid out the key things to consider when choosing your spot.

··2··
Try to have your patch facing north so that during winter when the sun is low on the northern horizon you still have plenty of sunlight.

··1··
There is a strong correlation between availability of sunlight and the success of growing food. We recommend 2–3 hours of sunlight per day for non-fruiting veggies (roots, leafy greens, brassicas, for example) and 4–6 for fruiting. This includes reflected and filtered sunlight.

Access to a water supply is pretty fundamental, so ensure you're within easy reach of a tap.

··4··

··3··
Stay away from large trees. They have far stronger root systems than your plants and will do anything they can to get the water they need. Some will also drop unwanted mess into your patch.

CHOOSING THE RIGHT POT

A trap for young players

Probably the most under-appreciated part of small-space gardening is choosing the correct-sized pot. A trap that many new gardeners fall into is buying a pot just big enough to accommodate the seedling they have bought.

Apart from saving space and being cheap, small pots are otherwise useless and destined to spectacularly fail. They dry out too quickly and give the plant no room to move. You need to let a plant be free and only then can it spread its wings.

The hardest thing in choosing a huge pot for a small seedling is how ridiculous it looks – worse than when your mum bought you a school uniform three sizes too big. But if you can overcome the laughter and humiliation, larger pots will give the plant more room to grow and let it soar like an eagle.

Such a simple way to get the most out of your plants.

··2··

Not only do small pots restrict the potential of your plant, but they also make life tough because the smaller the pot the quicker it dries out. Plants in small pots quickly become tired and root-bound.

··1··

Seems like the right fit – a small pot for a small plant.

Hey presto – a plant for life. Larger pots allow your plants to reach their full potential and contribute a truckload more produce to your table.

··3··

Planting a tiny seedling in a huge pot may appear a great waste of resources at first, but the larger the pot, the more your plant will grow.

··4··

ONE MINUTE SKILLS

CHASING THE SUN
Vertical gardens and raised beds

Just like the only way to get a better view of the band at a gig is to stand taller (or climb on your friend's shoulders), the only way for a garden to chase more sunlight is to plant it higher up. Vertical gardening is the solution for sun-starved city growers.

Any wall that basks in the glory of sunshine is a wall waiting to have things grown on it. It goes without saying that a green wall is a far better alternative than an empty one, giving you meaningful growing real estate in the most unlikely of places. If you live in a very urban environment, this may be your only available option.

In recent years modular systems have made wall gardening more accessible, allowing moderately handy people to create what appear to be grand feats of engineering. These systems allow you to easily dictate the size of your wall garden and you can add to the systems seamlessly when desired. And any wall will do, from timber to brick and even metal surfaces.

··1··

By elevating the height of the patch, you will get more access to sunlight. There are now more and more wall garden modules that cater perfectly to the job.

··2··

One limiting factor will be the height of the wall.

Another will be the ability to harvest. If it's not within arm's reach it's going to become tiresome to pick.

··3··

Sure you could use a ladder, but when a dish requires parsley that is a ladder-climb away you are more likely to not use parsley.

··4··

Vertical growing will allow you to grow food where you didn't think it was possible.

ONE MINUTE SKILLS

LINING A RECYCLED CRATE

Making a durable and drainable growing container

These days people prefer to use upcycled or salvaged items to do the job of the raised garden bed. Not only can you find priceless pieces of treasure perfectly suited to growing your food, but the materials also tend to come at a fraction of the price and are almost ready-made for the job.

Traditional raised garden beds are generally built to last out of durable materials. Generally, they are placed on soft landscapes so that water will drain through the existing soil structure. Salvaged or upcycled items – fruit bins, packing crates, storage units – are all contained and in most cases less than durable. They were not built for the purpose of holding large quantities of heavy, wet soil and this means a different set of rules applies to preparing them.

By preparing your veggie patch properly, your new-found treasure has a much greater chance of surviving to become a family heirloom.

··1··

Line the interior timber with thick plastic. This will prevent premature rotting. Don't line the bottom, making it watertight – it won't drain! Make sure the plastic is firmly stapled to prevent it from slipping. No-dig gardens have a habit of bringing down everything around them as their level falls.

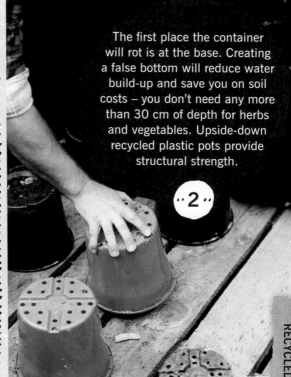

The first place the container will rot is at the base. Creating a false bottom will reduce water build-up and save you on soil costs – you don't need any more than 30 cm of depth for herbs and vegetables. Upside-down recycled plastic pots provide structural strength.

··2··

··3··

Some salvaged styrofoam boxes will help to fill in the gaps and are supported by the upside-down pots. Line the false bottom with weed matting to prevent soil from spilling through while allowing water to drain freely.

··4··

This veggie patch is destined for a long, happy and productive life.

TOP 5 ⟶

Easy-growers are an ego boost for all hopeless gardeners. This is gardening 101 and the only way you could fail growing these plants is by not trying to.

MINT

If you don't already have one, look to develop a drinking habit that peaks in summertime. Mojitos for all!

- Mint is suited to larger pots, at least 30 cm deep and 30 cm in diameter.
- **It loves water and isn't fussy for sunlight, so a damp, semi-shaded space – aka your B-spot – will do just fine.**
- When planting in a patch try to keep mint alone as it has a habit of interfering with others. In the right soil it's virtually impossible to over-water mint, so go for broke.
- **Mint is usually left alone by pests and disease, other than rust.**

SILVERBEET

Surplus is a given. Be prepared to lose friends by hounding them trying to offload excess silverbeet.

- Soak seeds in water overnight prior to planting, then sow directly into your patch or pot.
- **Silverbeet is suited to smaller pots, 15–20 cm deep. In a patch, plant seeds or seedlings 30–40 cm apart.**
- Apply liquid seaweed fertiliser once a fortnight. Keep well watered initially, approximately 2–3 times a week for the first month.
- **Silverbeet is a grazing green – simply snap off the outer leaves as you need them.**

EASY-GROWERS

RADISH

Vegetable gardening 101 starts with the radish. Pop them in the ground from seed, water and 6 weeks later you'll be sick of them.

- Radishes are suited to smaller, shallow pots. Plant seeds 5 cm apart.
- **Radishes can be planted at any time of year.**
- They will grow in most soil types, but prefer a friable and free-draining soil to allow room for easy root growth.
- **Apply phosphorous-rich blood and bone prior to planting.**
- Water 2–3 times a week over their lifetime to ensure roots are crisp and watery.

What makes it so easy to grow? We're certainly not smart enough to explain the evolution of the squash. Ask Darwin.

- Squash is best grown in an in-ground veggie patch. Plant seeds 1–1.5 m apart.
- **Squash will grow in most soil types but the soil must be free-draining. Mix through compost before planting.**
- Water 2–3 times a week until the plant is established (about a month), then cut back to once a week. Increase watering again when the plant fruits.
- **If growing a creeping variety, attach the plant to a trellis as it grows and pinch out growth tips (see page 90) to encourage it to branch out.**

SQUASH

SPRING ONION

Take a machete and chop them down to ground level and the buggers keep coming back! Some fear artificial intelligence; we fear the spring onion.

- Spring onion is suited to smaller pots. Plant seedlings 2–5 cm apart.
- **Spring onion can be planted at any time of year.**
- It will grow in most soil types, but prefers a free-draining, friable soil to allow room for easy root growth.
- **Apply liquid fertiliser every fortnight. Water about 3 times a week initially, then cut back to once a week.**
- Rather then ripping out the entire plant, chop it down to the base and it will regenerate (see page 140). Just don't leave them in-ground too long or they can become slimy.

TESTING YOUR SOIL FOR CONTAMINATES

It's always worth checking before planting

Cities, by nature, aren't the most sanitary of places. A walk down the streets of Collingwood or Kings Cross late on a Saturday night will confirm this. Cities are made up of homes and industry and all the people who inhabit them. The way we operate means the land below is not as pristine as we would hope. You can almost assume that the soil you are standing on is contaminated with something.

It may be hard to believe but these days cities take much better care of their soil than in years gone by. There are stricter codes governing building materials, the dumping of waste refuse and the general behaviour of people who live in cities, but that hasn't always been the case.

Most of the land we now consider the city was once probably farming land or industry – in a time without regulation or governance. Cities store the build-up of chemical waste and other hazardous materials in the soil. And this is the place you want to grow vegetables, so it always pays to check before planting!

ONE MINUTE SKILLS

PIMP YOUR SOIL

How to make the most of what you've got

Before starting a family you need to get the home that will accommodate them in order. Of course, that is not the way we all go about it, but if things are planned properly, getting the infrastructure right first will make looking after your family's needs easier. This is the kind of proactivity to use when it comes to your veggie patch family — before planting your vegetables you first need to focus on the growing soil that will house them.

Rather than gutting your home and building a new one, it makes sense to work with what you've got. Just a few minor adjustments and additions can turn any old abode into a royal family palace.

If you don't have a patch of earth to work with, and are using pots, tubs and boxes, you should use the best quality potting mix you can afford. If you do have some earth, you'll find that most existing soils will be largely devoid of nutrition and unable to harbour meaningful veggie life. Here are some ways to improve the soil quality of your patch.

2 Worms will eat organic matter and turn it into a product 10 times more fertile than before. Now those are some golden droppings! The castings not only hold valuable nutrition but are the conduit for plants to take up all the goodness that lies in the soil.

1 Compost will help restore imbalances in the pH level of your soil, provide nutrition for your plants and improve water retention.

3 Mulches such as pea straw, lucerne hay and sugar cane will introduce friability to the soil and allow it to breathe. They are also a valuable source of nutrition and protect the soil from baking hard under the sun.

4 Organic food scraps are another source of nutrition that will lure worms and other good organisms to work with you.

ONE MINUTE SKILLS

HOW MUCH COMPOST DO YOU NEED?

Let's talk numbers

At the end of a growing season your veggie patch is usually a little spent and in need of a makeover.

It has worked hard for months by growing and producing food for your table and this has drained its energy reserves. If it doesn't get another top-up of fuel, next season its output is going to fall. A pre-season energy boost is essential.

A complicated diet of chook manure, organic matter, synthetic fertilisers and the like is all well and good, but compost is a veggie patch's all-purpose energy bar and should be a staple for all your plants. While it helps refuel and improve your patch on so many levels it is also the one thing that you can produce at home, so using it liberally on your garden is a given.

Start of a new season: nutrition has been depleted, so time for a boost. But how much compost to use per m²?

1

2

One 25-L bag should be enough for 1 m² of veggie patch. Turn it through the top 10 cm of soil – don't dig down too deep as this will disrupt the organisms living in the soil.

Once dug through, level out evenly so that your blank canvas is prepared for planting.

3

Another season underway, full of promise.

4

HOW MUCH COMPOST DO YOU NEED?

27

ONE
MINUTE
SKILLS

GETTING THE pH LEVEL RIGHT

What to do if your soil is too alkaline or acidic

Another more technical idea of vegetable gardening is the way that the pH level in the soil can affect growing plants.

If soil is too alkaline or way too acidic, plants will simply not grow because they are unable to take up the nutrition in the soil. What we are constantly aiming for is a soil that hovers around slightly acidic to pH neutral. This range is going to accommodate the masses, allowing them to get a hit of what they're after. But that's not always what you get.

Our dry, clay-based soils tend to be very acidic. Conversely, the fresh soils you buy from a soil yard are usually alkaline. Rather than over complicating the phenomena and under explaining the solution, we prefer to accept this as fact and then find simple ways of solving the problem.

Doing a pH test isn't necessary if everything is fine and going well, but in cases where the usual 'get some rest and keep hydrated' doesn't work, a pH test is like a blood test for plants.

··1·· Soils and composts that come directly from the soil yard lean towards the alkaline side of things and need some adjustment.

··2·· Adding sulphur is a shock method that will help restore the pH to a neutral level.

··3·· Soils that are heavy in clay tend to be more acidic. These are generally established soils, rather than fresh ones.

The equal but opposite course of action to adding sulphur is using dolomite lime to lift the pH.

··4·· Using sulphur and lime are shock methods for persistent pH issues. Rather than jumping straight to them at the first sign of the problem, adding compost is the patient, incremental solution that will help restore parity.

ONE MINUTE SKILLS

TOPPING UP A NO-DIG GARDEN

A necessary evil

One thing we always struggle to find the time for is topping up a no-dig garden. It just seems so tedious and never feels like the 'right time'.

The problem is there's always something growing in the patch, whether a seasonal crop or perennial herb (one that lives for more than two years). The idea of ripping things out seems wasteful, but sacrifices may be needed. Shockingly, you may have to cut one life short for the benefit of others. But at least *you* get to play God, right?

To reduce wastefulness, plan your top-up to coincide with the change of seasons, which is usually at the end of a harvesting period. Mature perennial herbs won't be a problem as they are hardy enough to be transplanted. Make sure you give them water 20–30 minutes prior to surgery and dig out plenty of soil around the root zone. Then you can get started on topping up.

1

Depending on how sunken the patch is, a layer of pea straw, lucerne hay or sugar cane mulch may be necessary. If it has dropped by more than 30 cm, put in a 5–10 cm layer and sprinkle with a handful of pelletised organic fertiliser per m².

2

Now for the mushroom compost. This will make up the next 20 cm of the top-up. Make sure to compact the ingredients once they're in as there will be a lot of air in both the compost and mulch. This will lessen the next sinking.

3

Because the mushroom compost is too alkaline to plant straight into, top over with a bag of compost to balance out the pH. Finally, add a bag of good-quality potting mix and some worm castings.

4

Transplant the herbs back, making sure to soak them in immediately. The water requirements as they settle back in will be elevated. Although they may look sad initially, they will survive with the right care. Now you have a blank canvas and the next move is up to you!

ONE
MINUTE
SKILLS

EASY-PEASY TRELLISING

A quick guide to getting vertical

Cities are full of tall buildings that maximise precious real estate space.

Instead of lamenting modern-day construction, gardeners should be inspired by what is around them to maximise their yield in the veggie patch. This means growing plants vertically.

Of course, you need the right infrastructure to get your plants working on a higher level. A good trellising system is required.

It turns out the best trellising system we have found was never intended for the job. Rather than mess around with timber and bamboo and ancient building practices, this material has structural integrity, longevity, flexibility and, most importantly, it's a cinch to install.

It is now popping up all over the city!

1

It is often materials not originally intended for the job that make the best trellis – much like this concrete trench mesh bar. You can find them at landscape and building supply yards.

2

The entire 6 m length is easily malleable into a neatly presented arbour that requires almost no construction. Simply wedge or dig in one end of the mesh on one side and then carefully bend it and wedge it into the other. Once in place, secure.

3

Cut in half, it's the perfect length for an inner apple crate trellis. With less length and give, this will require more strength to fit in place. Wedge it in at one end, then bend it and secure to the other. This can also double as the infrastructure for netting or shade cloths.

4

Finally, we use flat metal saddles and screws to hold it in place.

ONE MINUTE SKILLS

What time of year to plant? **36**

What time of day to plant? **38**

How to soak hard-coated seeds **40**

How to plant seeds **42**

How to plant seedlings **48**

Easy incubator **52**

Spacing your plants **54**

Companion planting no-brainers **58**

How to plant garlic **60**

It's … tomato time! **62**

Crop rotation no-brainers **64**

TOP 5 → SHADE-LOVERS **46**

TOP 5 → CLIMBERS **56**

GET
planting

ONE
MINUTE
SKILLS

WHAT TIME OF YEAR TO PLANT?

Combine your instincts with available information

Advice for patch set-up and preparation, maintenance and care, and planting and harvesting times, is widespread and readily available. While these are the best guides for new gardeners to follow, they are only recommendations. Even something as particular as planting times are open to interpretation by every gardener.

We sometimes wonder at how many people appear rigidly programmed when it comes to planting out their patch – sitting patiently, staring at the calendar, waiting for the month to end before planting their tomato seeds. By saying this we don't mean to devalue general recommendations and a good routine; we are simply asking you to get a feel for your instincts and then begin to trust them.

2 Look at the weather you're currently experiencing and compare how in tune it is with the standard. Recommended planting times assume standardised weather patterns and don't account for unseasonal weather. It may be a hot start to spring and this will bring planting times forward.

1 Recommended planting times are the best guides, but don't feel the need to live too strictly by them.

3 The people who come up with recommended planting times don't know what sort of microclimate you have brewing in your yard.

Your north-facing brick wall may create an oven effect, allowing you to grow chillies well into winter.

4 Rather than strictly following the recommended planting times, be guided by them. Offbeat weather patterns and unique microclimates create all sorts of veggie-growing possibilities.

ONE
MINUTE
SKILLS

WHAT TIME OF DAY TO PLANT?

The ideal conditions for your plants (it's not all about you)

Your plants are so delicate and precious when young – they need to be treated properly so they get the best start in life.

As explained in 'How to plant seedlings' (page 48), young plants are already coping with a massive shock in their lives: stolen from a structured, organised life in a greenhouse they now have to cope with the reality of your garden and your erratic ways.

Choosing the right planting time shouldn't be seen as a massive sacrifice. We are not asking you to reorganise your life, it's just that this hour or so of work needs some thought and it will make the outcome more likely to go in your favour.

Okay, the seedlings are ready, but what about the weather?

·· 1 ··

·· 2 ··

While it feels so good to be in the garden planting out the patch on a hot sunny day, remember that sun and heat are the enemies of young seedlings. Combined they can cause real damage. Afternoon planting on a hot day is a big no-no.

Don't fancy rain and muddy hands? Unfortunately, these are the ideal planting conditions. Try to find a balance for your planting day. If it's going to be a stinker, get up and put them in early. That way you can water them in before the sun really strikes.

·· 3 ··

·· 4 ··

Giving your plants the best possible start in life will hold them in good stead for a long, fruitful future.

HOW TO SOAK
HARD-COATED SEEDS

Lending nature a helping hand

Working with nature means there will always be things out of your control and sometimes the success or failure of your plants may come down to no more than good fortune or bad luck. While we can't stop freak spring cold snaps or rogue tornados from causing havoc in the patch, there are some things within your control that put the question of luck further from the equation. Soaking seeds before planting is one such thing.

Some seeds, such as lettuce and broccoli, have a relatively soft outer shell that breaks down easily to allow for germination. On the other hand, there are tougher makes, such as peas and beans, which have a tough outer coating, and these can do with some help.

Soaking these types of seeds in water overnight prior to planting will not only soften the tough coating, it will also provide a useful store of water that the seed can draw on during the germination process.

··1··

The pea is one example of a seed with a hard exterior coating that will benefit from soaking prior to planting. Others include beans, broad beans, sweetcorn and beetroot.

··2··

Choose a jar, fill it with room temperature water and add your seeds. Only soak as many seeds as you want to plant, not the whole packet! Leave overnight.

If there are any seeds floating on the surface the next day, toss these out as they will be spoiled. Drain the rest of the seeds. The speed and chance of germination is now in your favour.

··3··

··4··

Your seeds are ready for planting. Soaked seeds hold moisture inside them, so rather than watering daily until germination, it's best to give them one large soak after planting then hold off watering until germination. Too much water now can cause rotting, making them susceptible to rodent night raids.

ONE
MINUTE
SKILLS

HOW TO PLANT SEEDS
Tips and tricks for maximum success

Open a pack of seeds and potential life comes spilling out. If you are in the habit of collecting your own seeds, then you know just how abundant these things are and how little they cost. For the average punter, a pack of seeds offers the best value and knowing how to use those seeds is an essential skill.

The seeds you select will hinge on a few important factors – what is in season, the amount of light the plants will receive and, of course, what you like to eat. If you don't like to eat lettuce, don't sow it. If you don't know what to grow, have a look over the neighbour's fence or ask them what they recommend.

Once you've settled on what to plant, it then becomes a matter of how, and there are some simple rules to follow.

1

Seeds come in all shapes and sizes and should be treated based on their characteristics.

a lovely soak

2

Larger seeds with a hard coating will benefit from a soak in water the night prior to planting (see page 40). This helps break down the tough coating and improve the chances of germination.

3

When it comes to planting depths, the rule of thumb is twice the depth of the seed's diameter. Therefore if a seed is 1 cm in diameter, it needs to be planted 2 cm below the soil.

4

Larger seeds are best sown in individual holes, in pairs – in case one doesn't germinate, you have backup! If both germinate, cull the weaker one once they get to a culling size. Make sure to sow to the required spacing of the variety.

⟫ CONTINUED OVERLEAF

ONE
MINUTE
SKILLS

GET PLANTING

5

Measuring seeds to determine what depth to plant them is fine for larger varieties, but what about seeds the size of a bee's tail? With these guys just plant them at a depth that prevents them from blowing away or being taken by birds. A dusting of soil will do.

6

Rather than precisely measuring tiny holes, create trench lines with the tip of your index finger at the necessary spacing.

7

It's going to be hard to precisely space in the trench line so just do your best and prepare yourself for some culling down the track.

8

After planting seeds, water them in using a fan spray. For larger varieties that have been soaked overnight and will be holding some water reserve, just water in once after sowing and hold back until germination. These seeds have the propensity to rot or get snacked on by rats.

The sun is a great thing but not everyone likes to bask in its full glory. Like your friend with pasty legs who never wears shorts, there are some plants that are a bit pasty too, and prefer a bit of cover.

Vietnamese mint is quite a shady character in itself so put it in a space that complements that.

- Vietnamese mint likes a decent-sized pot with room to move, about 30 cm in depth and diameter.
- **It can be grown at all times of the year but loves humid and warm conditions (reminds it of home).**
- If planting in the patch, be prepared for Vietnamese mint to take over. Try to isolate it when you can.
- **Lack of moisture is one problem, so keep the watering up, particularly when the plant is young.**

VIETNAMESE MINT

GARLIC

The best way to eat garlic (and turn off your partner) is as a whole head, roasted slowly, smudged on a piece of toast in the morning.

- Garlic is suited to smaller pots, with at least 20 cm in depth. Plant cloves 10–15 cm apart.
- **It prefers a free-draining, friable soil with compost. If the soil is compacted, the bulbs won't grow well.**
- Water 2–3 times a week initially, then cut back to once a week depending on the conditions.
- **Garlic has an extensive growing period, up to 9 months.**
- Garlic should be sown from the previous year's bulbs (see page 60), so save your best for planting the following season.

SHADE-LOVERS

LEMON BALM

Lemon balm can be used as a poor substitute for common or Vietnamese mint, but infused in drinks or ice cream it has a starring role.

- It'll grow in small pots, but it will grow better in big ones.
- **Lemon balm prefers partly to fully shaded spaces.**
- It grows best in warm, humid conditions but will make a go of it at most times of the year.
- **Problems like pests and sooty mould are more likely to be caused by the shaded environments you end up planting lemon balm in than by the plant itself.**

CORIANDER

Coriander gets all hot under the collar when it's too sunny and hot. It prefers a much milder environment.

- Coriander is ideally suited to pots. These should be roughly 20 cm in depth and diameter.
- **Coriander likes part shade in a light spot – like the shade that is so pleasant to find on a warm day.**
- Keep your plant well hydrated but ensure your soil drains adequately – coriander is prone to rotting when it can't dry out.
- **Bolting to seed is the biggest problem with coriander. If you catch it early enough, snipping off the seed head will force the plant to focus on leaf production again (see page 72). If you catch it too late, leave it and score some seeds for your spice cabinet.**

SORREL

Sorrel is custom-built for the kind of shade you find in a tiny backyard on the fringe of the CBD.

- Sorrel grows well in small spaces, so pots that are no more than 10–15 cm in depth and diameter will suffice.
- **Sorrel prefers early spring weather, but will tolerate just about anything the weather gods throw at it.**
- When sorrel gets stressed or too old it throws out big, tough seed heads and tough leaves to match. In this event, start over and plant new sorrel.
- **To keep sorrel from tasting like sour lemons, plant it closer together than is normally recommended – it stays more delicate and sweet this way.**

ONE MINUTE SKILLS

HOW TO PLANT SEEDLINGS

Planting seedlings is not just for the lazy, it's for the gardener who looks at their watch and decides 'I gotta bust a move!'

While propagating from seed is no doubt the most cost-effective way to grow your food, when you enter the season late or simply don't have the time to invest, you can always fall back on the seedling. And thankfully, some well-organised nursery has grown it on your behalf.

Despite the apparent ease of planting seedlings, there are traps that both the experienced and inexperienced gardener can fall into. A first-timer pitfall is planting the whole lot together and then finding them stunted and struggling a month down the track. Old hands may just be more preoccupied with their tea break than some important hydration for the plant prior to planting.

2 These guys have spent the formative months of their lives in a cosy greenhouse and now they come face to face with reality. They are no doubt thirsty, tired and worried. Make it a pleasant transition by watering the seedlings 10 minutes before transplanting.

1 The chosen ones for the transplant.

3 The first trap is planting all the seedlings together, unaware that there are tens of seedlings in the punnet that all need separating.

4 When transplanting, first break off the excess roots at the base.

CONTINUED OVERLEAF

GET PLANTING

5

In terms of herbs, some can be planted in one hit, such as rosemary, thyme, sage and oregano. Other herbs, such as chives, basil, coriander, dill and parsley, should be divided into segments. Be careful when breaking off segments to minimise damage to the roots and foliage.

6

Rectangular punnets present neatly organised seedlings. Separation of these is more straightforward. Pinch each seedling out, clearing off any excess root growth.

7

Square punnets present the greatest challenge – a ton of tiny seedlings, all crammed into a tight space, needing separation. Usually any plant grown in this fashion can cope being planted with a partner, but you will get the most out of them if each is separated.

8

Now time to plant away and water in.

ONE MINUTE SKILLS

EASY INCUBATOR

Give your seedlings some extra TLC

There are some moves into the patch that are more delicate than others and with these cases extra sensitivity is required. If you are planting a seedling before its optimum time, a little cover will help it get through a tricky cooler period.

To improve the chances of a seedling's survival, we use temporary incubation to provide a home more consistent with the one it's just come from. It makes the transplant less of a shock and doubles as a barrier for pests.

Incubating seedlings is a method used in early spring as an insurance against dodgy weather. It's simple and straightforward and it only takes a piece of common household rubbish to do the job.

··1··

The tools for this job: an old soft drink bottle, a pair of scissors and our favourite variety of eggplant.

Choose a bottle large enough to allow the seedling to grow for the coming weeks, while incubation is necessary. Taking care, cut off the base of the soft drink bottle. Incubator complete.

··2··

Eggplant seedlings don't cope well with cold nights early on in the spring, so incubating is a good way of getting them growing in the patch early.

··3··

··4··

Place the incubator over the eggplant seedling with the cap off so it can breathe. When you get past the period of potential cold nights the incubator can come off and the eggplant is free!

ONE MINUTE SKILLS

SPACING YOUR PLANTS

Sometimes rules are made to be broken

Some people do what they are told to do and if the instructions on a punnet of seedlings say 'space seedlings every 20 cm' that is what they will do. Even though there may be seedlings left over they'd prefer to give them away or chuck them in the compost bin before questioning the authority on the matter.

You need to realise that these are only recommendations and straying a little won't land you in the naughty corner. It's also worth remembering that labels are pretty small, and if there was the luxury of space the instructions would probably read: ideally plant every 20 cm, but it's possible to have them as close as 15 cm or as wide apart as 25 cm, and if you choose to plant them every 30 cm, good luck to you, you may have the perfect soil and ideal spot for them to outshine our efforts.

They may also read: plant more than is necessary in the space you have so that, if some fail you have others to fall back on. This is called a backup plan.

Most labels on seedling punnets are kind enough to give you spacing information. These are your best guides to planting out the patch. **··1··**

Because we all like diversity in the patch but often don't have much space, the number of seedlings we buy generally will not fit to the suggested spacing. **··2··**

Rather than throw out or give away excess seedlings, plant more than is necessary. We like to do twice as much – half the spacing – as a contingency if some things don't take. This is not an ideal world we live in. **··3··**

If they all take they will inevitably start to crowd each other out. At that point you will need to cull the excess. Instead of throwing them in the compost bin, eat them young or give them away! **··4··**

TOP 5 ⟶

In the city, as in the garden, there is a constant battle to find some space and rise above the rabble. Some people build skyscrapers, while others plant vegetables that grow vertically. Beanstalk or Burj, both maximise the use of precious real estate by going tall.

PEAS

No amount of pea plants will ever be sufficient for your pea needs. Always keep a bag of frozen ones handy.

- Peas are suited to medium-sized pots, but prefer an in-ground veggie patch. Space plants 5–10 cm apart.
- **Some pea varieties grow well in spring but most prefer the cooler months.**
- Prior to planting, don't overload your soil with nitrogen, as peas produce it in abundance. Your plant will, however, appreciate an application of potash as it begins to flower.

BEANS

For climbers, you can't beat beans. There's a reason why Jack's co-star was a beanstalk.

- Beans are suited to larger pots, but prefer an in-ground veggie patch. Space plants 15–20 cm apart:
- **Beans fix your soil with nitrogen, which they produce naturally, so a moderately fertile, free-draining soil is required. If you can, plant them where you have just grown brassica crops, such as broccoli, cabbage or cauliflower.**
- Apply compost prior to planting. As the plants begin to flower, they will benefit from an application of potash.
- **Water seedlings around 2–3 times a week for the first month. Water twice a week when flowering, otherwise once a week for mature plants should do it.**

CLIMBERS

CUCUMBER

An average plant will reap you 30–50 cucumbers over a season. If you've developed a fondness for cucumber-infused gin and tonics you may need more plants.

- Cucumbers are suited to larger pots but prefer an in-ground veggie patch. Space plants 50 cm apart, ideally on a trellis.
- Feed your plants fortnightly with an application of liquid seaweed fertiliser. Water 2–3 times a week for the first month, then cut back to once a week (or twice if it's hot).
- As your plant begins to mature, pinch out the growth tips to encourage it to branch out and produce more cucumbers (see page 90).

A well-trained climbing spinach plant is almost closer to a piece of art than a piece of food.

CLIMBING SPINACH

- Climbing spinach can be grown in larger pots, but as a rigorous grower it will prefer an in-ground position to sink its teeth into.
- It will grow well at most times of the year but really thrives in cooler conditions.
- The steel mesh sheets used to reinforce concrete couldn't be better designed for growing climbing spinach on.
- Climbing spinach is not going to be a kitchen staple for most – it looks almost like a succulent and the leaves can be quite slimy (leave your plants in-ground too long and they'll get even slimier). One or two plants will provide plenty of opportunity for that special occasion.

PUMPKIN

One well-grown, well-pollinated vine will make you more than enough pumpkin soup.

- Pumpkin is best grown in spring, in an in-ground veggie patch. Space plants 1.5 m apart.
- Prepare your soil with compost and manure to help with the plant's initial growth. It will benefit from an application of potash as it begins to flower.
- Briefly water 3–4 times a week initially, then cut back to a couple of good soakings each week as it begins to mature.
- Pumpkin has problems with pollination, so you may need to hand-pollinate to increase the likelihood of fruit setting (see page 94). Put some good music on, get in the mood.

ONE
MINUTE
SKILLS

COMPANION PLANTING NO-BRAINERS
Romeo and Juliet, Beyonce and Jay-Z, Onion and Strawberry

Some plants get along, but some plants *really* get along, and these are the ones that should be hanging out together in your veggie patch. Put them alongside one another and love burns. One may attract a beneficial insect to pollinate the other, or fix the soil with fuel that the other needs, or just thrill the other in a way we as humans fail to understand. Whatever the reason, some plants just belong together.

Companion planting is an old farming principle that has been used for centuries. Rather than using fertilisers or pesticides to maintain the land, companion planting is used to maximise all that nature has to offer.

More relevant to larger scale farming than small-space gardening, the main strategy of companion planting at home is to encourage diversity, particularly through the use of herbs and flowers. There are, however, some plants that are meant to live alongside each other – these are the no-brainers.

1 Strawberries and onions get along great. Onions do the strawberries a huge favour by repelling slugs, which often eat the strawberries before you do. Plant your onions in and around your strawberries, no closer than 20 cm. It works with the entire allium family – chives, garlic, spring onions etc.

2 Sweetcorn grows tall and gives climbing beans something to grow on – a living trellis of sorts. Beans fix the soil with nitrogen, which sweetcorn needs in spades. Timing here is crucial. Plant your beans a month after the sweetcorn, 20 cm away from the stems.

3 Tomato and basil just get along. That's all you need to know. Plant basil in and around your tomato plants.

4 The nasturtium is every veggie's friend and will attract pollinators and deter pests. We like to grow them around the fringes of our patch – kind of a welcome and warning all in one.

STILL WANT MORE?
WHY NOT TRY:
→
• Beetroot with lettuce
• Eggplant with spinach
• Carrot with radish
• Leek with celery

ONE MINUTE SKILLS

HOW TO PLANT GARLIC

Getting more bang for your buck

One basic principle of vegetable gardening is that from one very cheap seed you can grow a big, bountiful plant that is worth a hell of a lot more. The same applies across the board, whether growing from a runner, cutting or a bulb of garlic. It's therefore a little surprising how many people believe that to grow one bulb of garlic it takes exactly … one bulb of garlic.

In a world where you would hope for a minimum of 5% yield on investments, a one-for-one swap is one of the poorest returns on the market. In fact, it is worse than a poor return because no return exists at all. It would be like upgrading an old phone for the same one.

Of course, there is a better return to be had from your one bulb of garlic and it starts with breaking it up into cloves.

··1··

The value begins with breaking the bulb into cloves – 1, 2, 3 ... this is getting better.

··2··

If you've ever left garlic too long in the cupboard you will know it sprouts green shoots and that's exactly what will happen once the cloves are put underground. Don't be foolish and bury them upside down.

Plant the clove to the same depth as its height – that is, if the clove is 2 cm in height, bury it 2 cm deep – cover over and water in. And wait.

··3··

··4··

12 cloves = 12 bulbs ... in about 9 months' time, that is.

ONE MINUTE SKILLS

IT'S ... TOMATO TIME!

When to plant different tomato varieties

We don't need to remind you how much we love tomato season, but we will. We love tomato season. We love it more than all the other times of the year *put together*. We probably even love it more than the tomato itself because there are some rare things in life where the anticipation of an event is actually better than the event itself.

More than any other vegetable the tomato is most important culturally and personally. It's responsible for the creation of our business and it's what gets us out of bed in the morning – even after too many Bloody Mary's – and so holding onto the season for as long as possible is vital.

Not all tomatoes are the same and not all tomatoes like the same conditions. Some cope better with a long summer, just as others will appreciate more spring-like conditions. What this all points to is that certain varieties are more suited to certain times of the year, so to make the good times last, you need to get your variety timings right.

WHOOP, WHOOP!

1

Our favourite time of the year: tomato planting.

2

The advice we give to those in temperate climates is to plant your seedlings in the patch on Melbourne Cup Day (or near enough!). If you can't wait and want to get something in a little earlier, choose smaller, cherry-style varieties as these are good early-season performers.

3

Come Melbourne Cup Day or later, the larger varieties – for example, Black Russian and Burnley Surecrop – are more suited.

4

Staggering the planting with the most suited varieties will make for a longer harvesting period and more extensive good times. Why deny it?

ONE MINUTE SKILLS

CROP ROTATION NO-BRAINERS

Making the most of your patch

There are few no-brainers in life. Only a handful spring to mind ... Cheap movie Mondays: it is a Monday, movies are half price and it is the perfect opportunity for a cheap date. No-brainer.

Coffee at your local: need coffee, great coffee, cute staff. No-brainer.

Not drinking orange juice after brushing your teeth. No-brainer.

Crop rotation: seasonal planting rotations that provide synergy all year round. No-brainer.

Crop rotation is one rock only the foolish leaved unturned. In small-space gardening you really need to exploit every trick at your disposal and this is one technique that helps make the most of your precious real estate by managing the needs of your plants. It helps alleviate fertilising and maximises what the plant gives you back in return. And it just feels 'right'.

Sometimes it is not just the harvest a plant provides – it's the potential for future harvests the next season and beyond. Smart crop rotation guarantees that.

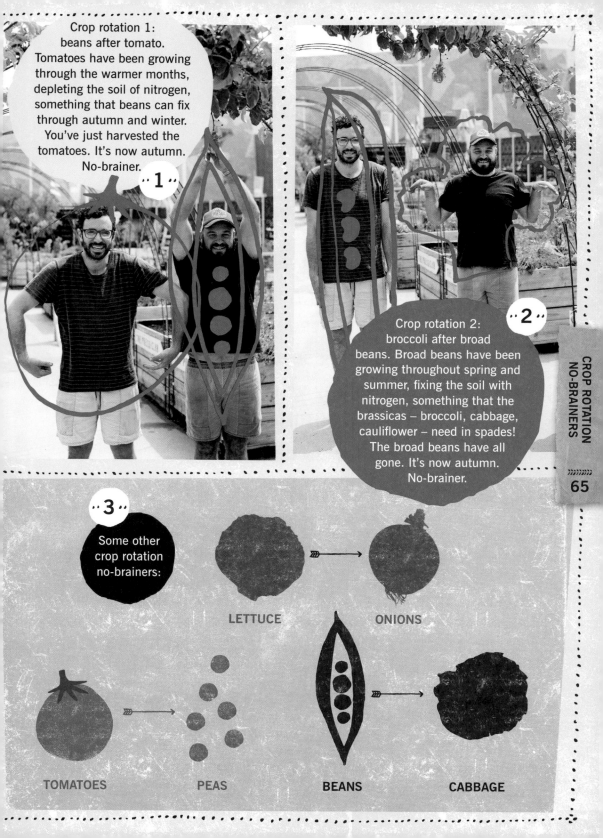

Crop rotation 1: beans after tomato. Tomatoes have been growing through the warmer months, depleting the soil of nitrogen, something that beans can fix through autumn and winter. You've just harvested the tomatoes. It's now autumn. No-brainer.

Crop rotation 2: broccoli after broad beans. Broad beans have been growing throughout spring and summer, fixing the soil with nitrogen, something that the brassicas – broccoli, cabbage, cauliflower – need in spades! The broad beans have all gone. It's now autumn. No-brainer.

Some other crop rotation no-brainers:

LETTUCE → ONIONS

TOMATOES → PEAS

BEANS → CABBAGE

ONE
MINUTE
SKILLS

The best time to water your patch 68

Too much or not enough? 70

Picking seed heads 72

Culling seedlings 74

Why fan-spray watering is best 78

How to fertilise in pots 80

How to mulch 82

Pruning fruit trees 86

The art of pinching 90

Staking tomatoes like a pro 92

Hand-pollination for beginners 94

Pruning raspberries 98

Transplanting strawberry runners 100

TOP 5 ➤ SMALL-SPACE PLANTS 76

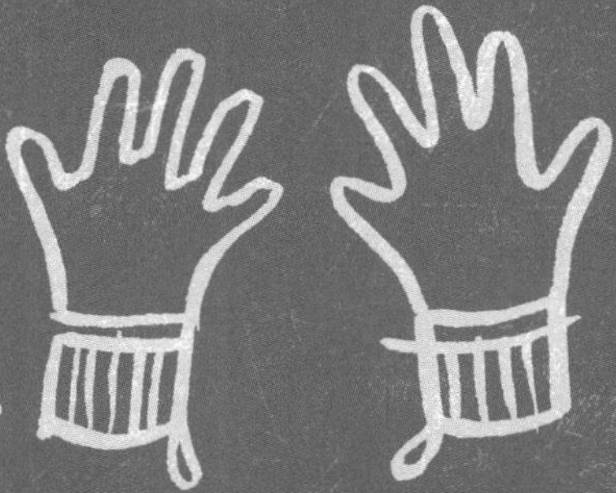

and pot!

PATCH

love

ONE
MINUTE
SKILLS

THE BEST TIME TO WATER YOUR PATCH

Watering is so fundamental that many people wouldn't even consider it to be a skill.

They couldn't be more wrong. Good watering practices help to foster healthy plants and keep pests and disease at bay … as long as it's timed right.

With the exception of very hot days, only water plants first thing in the morning. This way they can draw a supply of water throughout the day when they need it most. While people may enjoy a refreshing drink in the evening, watering plants at that time will only encourage pests to find a home in your patch.

Like a strong latte or hay fever tablet, make watering part of your morning routine.

1

Damn that tastes good, and it feels so 'right'. An afternoon beer and afternoon watering go hand in hand.

2

Plants don't use water at night. Leaving the patch wet at sundown means it remains wet throughout the night. Most pests operate in the dark of the night and are attracted to moisture. This kind of watering will create the perfect patch party for hoards of uninvited guests.

3

That's more like it, a good soaking in the morning, with cuppa in hand.

4

Watering in the morning will allow the plants to take up moisture as they need it during the day.

ONE
MINUTE
SKILLS

TOO MUCH OR NOT ENOUGH?

Let's make one thing clear: it's not that you kill plants, it's just that you don't water them.

There is no such thing as green or black thumbs. When it comes down to it, there are two types of people – those who water their plants and those who don't.

Knowing how much to water plants is no more complicated than realising you need to apply the brakes when your car approaches a red light.

Happy plants that are receiving the required dose of water. It's easy to see that this patch is THRIVING.

·· 1 ··

·· 2 ··

Plants can often 'play dead' on a excessively hot days in an attempt to reduce their surface area and exposure to the sun. But a plant that looks like this on a mild/warm day is trying to tell you something – 'water me!'.

Regular neglect, through insufficient or sporadic watering, will leave a plant dying from the outside in. There is not enough water to sustain the older, mature growth, only enough to sprout new shoots.

·· 3 ··

·· 4 ··

In the rarer circumstance of receiving too much water, plants will become susceptible to fungal diseases, particularly sooty mould. This usually happens because there is not enough sunlight to dry out your garden. Holding back on the water and letting it breathe is the best course of action.

ONE MINUTE SKILLS

PICKING SEED HEADS

Nipping problems in the bud

Lettuces and other leafy greens can develop seed heads for a number of reasons, and other than for the purpose of collecting and saving seeds, they are not particularly welcome in the veggie patch.

But that's okay. This is just another problem requiring a solution and the first part is in understanding why the plants develop seed heads in the first place.

Seed heads develop through stress – mainly because of our negligence – so when a plant decides that they're stressed the natural inclination is to shoot a seed head skyward and fly the white flag. It's their way of saying, 'It's been fun, but I'm out of here'.

Regardless of whether the stress is caused by transplant shock, lack of picking or the natural conclusion of their life cycle, it is up to you to set things back on track. Picking seed heads helps to do that.

The holiday/lazy gardener seed head, caused by people who take too many holidays or are too lazy during the harvesting period to pick their food. Obviously more important things to do with their time …

1

The transplant shock seed head, caused by the rude awakening of stepping into your patch from a cosy environment!

2

3

The natural end-of-life seed head. Just something that we have to get used to – it's going to happen to all of them one day.

Pinch seed heads out at the next junction of useful leaves. Sharp nails are required for tough seed heads such as those on rocket, so perhaps use scissors to reduce any collateral damage. Now the plant can get on with more useful things like growing food.

4

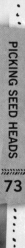

ONE MINUTE SKILLS

CULLING SEEDLINGS

Sometimes you have to be cruel to be kind

Each year more than 2 million kangaroos are killed in our country and almost no-one blinks an eye. Yet ask someone to cull a perfectly healthy tomato seedling and they are likely to cry murder!

You've done the hard work – you saved the seeds from last season's best plant, you sowed them under the full moon and did the sacred rain dance ... or perhaps you spilled a pack of seeds onto the ground and forgot what you planted. Boy, gardening sure is easy. No matter how you got there, the seedlings are growing and there are a lot of them. The bad news is that you will have to cull a few at the peak of their potential.

This is one of those situations in which 'less is more'. It is tough to do, but – for the greater good – it is a job that must be done.

1

You need to cull before the plants' roots become entangled – otherwise the removal of one plant will damage and possibly kill the other. Similarly, leaving them together will mean they are in constant competition for water and sunlight.

2

These seedlings are just the right size to separate – healthy, yet not large enough to have extensive root systems. Brace the seedling you wish to keep, holding it firmly but not crushing it. With the other hand, grab the adjacent seedling, lightly jiggling and pulling it from the ground.

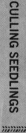

3

Be as sentimental as you want once the seedlings are out of the ground. Whether you sing a song and put a candle in your window, or simply toss the seedlings into the compost is up to you.

4

Bigger plants such as zucchini or tomato may need a few rounds of culling as they mature. If the feeling of waste is overwhelming, offer these extras to your neighbours or friends.

Never an imposition and always welcomed with open arms, these are the fruit and veggies you always want in your patch. They don't take up much space and their needs are fairly basic ... the ultimate houseguests, really.

Lettuces like their own kind. Put them among a strange crowd and they usually retreat into their shells.

- Lettuces are suited to small, shallow pots. Space plants 10–20 cm apart.
- **Lettuces can be planted at any time of year.**
- Prepare your soil with compost and manure prior to planting. Leafy greens need plenty of nitrogen to sustain leaf growth, so try for fortnightly, even weekly, applications of liquid fertiliser.
- **Water seedlings daily for the first 2 weeks, then cut back to 2–3 times a week.**

LETTUCE

HERBS

Never pay $3 for a sprig of rosemary again ...

- Rosemary is ideal for pot growing – it's why pots were invented!
- **As discussed in 'Choosing the right pot' (page 14), the return on your herbs positively correlates to the size of your pot.**
- Plant rosemary in full sun.
- **There are some annual herbs, such as basil and coriander, but most (like rosemary) are perennial and can be planted year-round. They prefer the beginning of spring for the best possible start but any other stage of the year, apart from the depths of winter, is okay.**

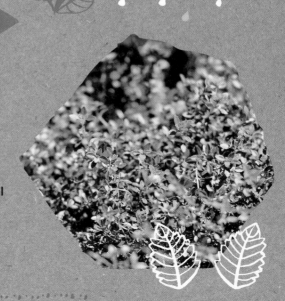

SMALL-SPACE PLANTS

STRAWBERRY

Strawberries are tasty and expensive, so well worth the effort of growing.

- Strawberries are suited to smaller pots, roughly 20 cm in depth and diameter. In a patch, space plants 20 cm apart.
- **Dig through compost and manure before planting.**
- Strawberries can be planted at any time of year, but prefer to establish at the peaks of spring and autumn.
- **Water 2–3 times a week for the first month and avoid overwetting the foliage, as this will make it susceptible to fungal diseases.**

For the quickest return in the veggie-growing world (that isn't a leafy green), you can't go past the radish.

- Radishes are suited to small, shallow pots. Space plants 5 cm apart.
- **They can be planted at any time of year, but prefer spring.**
- Excessive nitrogen will result in prolific leaf growth at the expense of root growth, so don't overfertilise. A fortnightly application of liquid seaweed fertiliser will suffice. Water 2–3 times a week over their lifetime to ensure the roots do not split.
- **The flavour of the root tends to develop with time, so those left to mature will generally be spicier. But beware of letting them go too long as they can become tough and fibrous.**

RADISH

POTATO

The potato may seem out of place in this list, but growing it in a potato tower demands little of your patch real estate.

- Source your potato seeds from a reputable supplier to ensure they are disease free.
- **Potatoes are best grown at the beginning of spring and autumn. Use compost as the growing medium.**
- Water once or twice a week over their lifetime.
- **It's best to grow potatoes in a tower, adding new levels as the foliage grows. Covering over the foliage encourages more tuber development and more potatoes. When the third or fourth level has grown and then started to die back, it's time to harvest.**

ONE
MINUTE
SKILLS

WHY FAN-SPRAY WATERING IS BEST

Try a little tenderness

We shouldn't need to say it, but plants prefer to be watered rather than attacked.

Blasting your patch with a jet stream hose is not considered a drink – probably more like a bombing. It's no better than throwing pumpkins at a group of hungry people with no arms to shield themselves or legs to run.

A garden hose is great – don't get us wrong – but the nozzles are expensive and break often. Instead, everybody should own a 9-litre plastic watering can with a fan spray. They cost about $10, they're indestructible, they carry a good amount of water for small-space patches and they give the plants a drink how they like it.

As a bonus, having a measured device lets you know how much water you're giving your plants and so allows you to distribute in a measured way.

1
These little guys are most sensitive to abusive methods of watering.

2
POW! It's hard to know what we're trying to achieve here. Some would say 'water', but it could well be a new technique of serving up fresh veggies, dislodged straight from the patch onto your plate.

The carnage. Such a sad sight, particularly because they were so tedious to sow in the first place. All that is left are seeds and seedlings exposed to the elements.

3

4
The fan spray: gentle, thorough and sensitive to the needs of your patch. We like to use one full watering can per veggie crate for immature plants (twice a day), and three watering cans 2 or 3 times a week when we up the ante. Weather dependent, of course.

ONE MINUTE SKILLS

HOW TO FERTILISE IN POTS

Hint: it's a little bit like cooking

Any bag of fertiliser you use will have an application rate that is tailored for in-ground plants, so what happens when you apply the same amount to your potted varieties?

First think of your in-ground plants as sitting on top of a vast ocean of soil. Whatever is applied to this ocean, some will be taken up by the plants on the surface, but a lot will dissipate throughout. It is a little different for your plants sitting in a pot.

The problem with applying fertiliser to potted plants is it all stays in the pot at a higher concentration and much more is taken up by the plant. While that may seem like a good thing, good things can be overdone, just like when you went overboard on the last cheese fondue. Too much cheese is not so different from too much fertiliser for a plant – it will send you all yellow around the edges.

Fertilising potted plants is best done incrementally, in moderation.

1 The back of any fertiliser pack will reveal the application per m². When fertilising in a vast ocean of soil, the instructions on the pack will be just right.

2 The little pool of soil in our pot, all contained and with nowhere else to go. The biggest blunder is applying the same rate per m² as indicated on the pack.

3 Just like when you're cooking, you can put the salt in but you can't take it out – start small and taste.

4 Use your eyes and see how the plant reacts. You can always add more!

ONE MINUTE SKILLS

HOW TO MULCH

If you're going to do it, do it right

Just like 'Google', 'mulch' is one of those rare noun/verbs that forever changes and redefines cultures and civilisations. Mulching is very, very important.

From lucerne to sugar cane, pea straw to wood chips, mulching is gardening's silver bullet. It helps regulate soil temperature, keeps in moisture, suppresses weeds and, as mulch breaks down, it provides valuable food for your plants.

While we harp on about mulching, the message often gets lost. Perhaps it comes down to complacency: why mulch a patch that is doing well without it? Because mulching is what turns a honeymoon into a marriage – mulching will make it last.

1

The three hotshots that all add nutritional value to the veggie patch as they break down. When mulching, make sure you use one of these.

EASY

DIFFICULT

2

Mulch comes in two forms — easy to apply or extremely tedious. Pulverised forms of mulch are always much easier to negotiate around your delicate seedlings whereas non-pulverised mulch is coarse and clumsy and will frustrate the hell out of you.

Mulch as soon as your seedlings are large enough to negotiate. When seedlings are too young there's every chance you'll smother them. When seedlings are too old, the soil may have crusted on the surface and become impervious to water.

3

4

Lay it on right.

CONTINUED OVERLEAF

ONE
MINUTE
SKILLS

Snug as a bug
in a rug ...

5 Too thin a layer and weeds will get through and water retention will be less than optimal.

6 Too thick a layer and you'll end up compromising your plants and prohibiting water from penetrating the patch.

7 The most precise measurement of mulch depth we have – the finger. Anywhere between the first and second knuckle will be just fine.

JUST RIGHT!

8 With larger plants – particularly capsicum, tomato and eggplant – keep a little breathing room around the stem to reduce the risk of stem rot.

ONE MINUTE SKILLS

PRUNING FRUIT TREES

Some basic concepts explained

Edward Scissorhands has been both a good and bad influence on the world of tree pruning.

For stylistic pruning – figs and other ornamental trees – he has been a huge inspiration. But when it comes to the pruning of fruit trees, his artistic approach does not translate well.

The most basic concept of pruning is that cutting back your tree will promote new growth, and that's a good thing. The next is to do with determining shape, and rather than sculpting rabbits or fairies, the shape of your tree needs to be geared for production purposes. It should be strongly defined and have good airflow.

Finally, the timing – when is the right time to prune your fruit trees? There are a couple of differing opinions on this, but one thing we can all agree on is not immediately after watching the film.

1 Scissorhands is at it again and he's using those trimmers like they were made for the job! Can't blame him ... that looks like fun. Promoting new growth is a two-steps-forward and one-step-back approach – you lose a little to get back a little bit more.

2 Prune after the tree has fruited. That means once a year for deciduous and some evergreen, but citrus that fruits twice a year will need two prunes.

CONTINUED OVERLEAF

ONE
MINUTE
SKILLS

·3·

Whether you are after a tall, slim tree or a wide, bushy one, always prune at a bud junction. To encourage the plant to grow tall cut at a bud that is heading skyward.

·4·

To encourage the plant to branch out, cut where the bud is pointing sideways.

This beautiful specimen has been pruned in recent years to encourage it to branch out.

·5·

·6·

This beautiful specimen was pruned very similarly to the other in its initial years of life but more recently has been encouraged to grow skyward. Both have uniquely different shapes yet both are strongly defined with good airflow throughout for fruit production.

PATCH (AND POT) LOVE

88

If your citrus is attacked by gall wasp don't prune out every new piece you come across. Citrus can live with gall wasp, but over time it does affect fruit production. Citrus should be cut back just before the larvae hatch in early spring. Place the pruning in the bin, not your green waste. This will minimise the spread of the pest.

··7··

··8··

Deciduous fruit trees develop fruit only on new growth, therefore seasonal pruning is essential for fruit production. Trim back last year's growth by 25–50%. You'll have new fruit and continued growth. For trees that are full size, cut back most of last season's growth.

Voila! New season fruit on new season growth.

ONE
MINUTE
SKILLS

THE ART OF PINCHING
And why we think it's necessary

To pinch or not to pinch, that is the question. Many believe Shakespeare was plagued by the pinching conundrum, and it remains an important question in today's veggie patch. Which side of the fence you sit on seems to hinge on the philosophical question: *is less ever more?*

Proponents of *more is more* believe that by not pinching out growth you get more plant with more opportunities to form fruit. Surely only a fool would deny a plant the chance to reach its full potential. So why pinch?

Pinching enthusiasts – we fall into that category – know that by pinching out the growth tips perhaps you get fewer flowers and, in theory, less fruit, but the fruit that develops is a superior breed and more likely to reach maturity.

We suggest you pinch … if you know what's good for you.

1 Rather than going on a random pinching mission, know what you need to pinch. At the junction of the stem and branch will be small shoots: we are going to pinch these out.

2 Not pinching makes a plant busier and bushier and less able to cope with fruit production. It reduces airflow and results in a plant that is less defined.

3 Pinch like a pro using your thumb and forefinger to remove the shoots. You could use scissors or secateurs but that wouldn't be pinching …

4 A plant that has been pinched is stronger, tougher, better looking and more able to cope with fruit production.

5 The same pinching theory applies to other plants such as pumpkins, peas and cucumbers. In these cases pinch out the tendrils.

ONE
MINUTE
SKILLS

STAKING TOMATOES
LIKE A PRO

Or, like Nonno

You have saved your seeds from the last season, propagated them in your custom-built greenhouse, prepared your soil the way they like it and then given them a homecoming.

No doubt you now deserve a holiday, or at the very least a commemorative medal, but a tomato's work is never done – all will be in vain without the right staking system.

Do you know the saying 'there are many ways to skin a cat'? Well, that makes no sense to us but there are plenty of ways that you can stake tomatoes. We have come across single, dual, triangular, even quadrangular systems. What is certain is that the way we stake tomatoes has evolved across generations and has been heavily influenced by our elders.

Who knows how far this method goes back? It has crossed at least two great oceans to find itself on these pages. Mastering it will get you closer to level 2 Italian credentials.

1 A tomato should be staked immediately after planting when there's less potential for damaging the root zone and before it has the chance to misshape. Let the plant's roots grow too large and you'll do damage when driving in the stakes. We favour the triangle stake method ...

2 Start by driving in your stakes, making sure they are well spaced and upright. A mature plant holding fruit will carry some weight so they'll need to be secure. It'll also make twining it far easier.

3 Use soft twine and tightly wrap it around the triad of stakes, starting from the bottom and working your way to the top. Each time you go around a stake, wrap it back on itself to prevent it from slipping.

There are purpose-built systems that work terrifically, are straightforward to install and can be used for years on end. If you're not interested in earning your Italian credentials, these are for you.

4 It's useful, but not essential, to have a small stake for the plant to hold onto before the staking. Take a moment to admire your work. Perfect.

5

ONE
MINUTE
SKILLS

HAND-POLLINATION
FOR BEGINNERS
Parental Guidance Recommended

Plants such as zucchini, pumpkin and squash can have trouble attracting the right kind of attention. When their flowers aren't pollinated properly, their fruit won't set. This means a helping hand may be required to finish what nature leaves unattended.

Despite the mutually beneficial outcome for both plant and grower, hand-pollination feels a little naughty. Try to remember that hand-pollination is a great way of ensuring a bountiful harvest, so there should be no reservations about this task.

There are a number of reasons why nature can fall short. Most are the direct consequence of inclement weather, when strong winds or great rainfalls can put pollinators off their game, but of more concern for inner city growers is a lack of pollinators in your patch.

But with the peace of mind that comes from knowing even the Pope hand-pollinates, it's about time we showed you how to do it properly.

1

Poor pollination is a problem that affects many plants but only certain varieties can be remedied with a bit of the old hand-pollination – these include pumpkin, squash, rockmelon, watermelon and, of course, our hero zucchini.

⟫ CONTINUED OVERLEAF

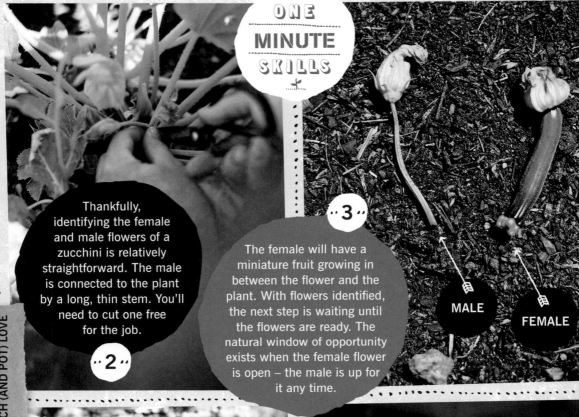

ONE
MINUTE
SKILLS

Thankfully, identifying the female and male flowers of a zucchini is relatively straightforward. The male is connected to the plant by a long, thin stem. You'll need to cut one free for the job.

··2··

··3··

The female will have a miniature fruit growing in between the flower and the plant. With flowers identified, the next step is waiting until the flowers are ready. The natural window of opportunity exists when the female flower is open – the male is up for it any time.

MALE

FEMALE

··4··

First put on some nice music to set the mood.

··5··

Now start the process by peeling back the male flower, exposing the stamen.

·6·

Rub the exposed stamen over the stigma in the female flower. Now you're hand-pollinating! You're really doing it!

·7·

You want to make sure the flower is properly fertilised so that the fruit sets. Remember you can't over-pollinate a flower, so hand-pollinate to your heart's content, or until you get bored.

ONE
MINUTE
SKILLS

PRUNING RASPBERRIES

It's easier than you think

Nature has a knack of growing berries in the wild with ease.

Hit any country road in late summer and you will find jungles of mess filled with delicious, ripe fruit lining the roadsides. It is a sight for sore eyes and one often greeted with suspicion – surely these delicious, ripe, tasty berries must be poisonous?

Berries grow so well in the wild because it is endowed with space; space that as home-growers we probably don't have. Growing berries at home needs to be more organised.

While at first glance berry plants seem like a bundle of random vines, there is order among them. Rather than cutting randomly in hope, there needs to be some order when you are pruning them, too.

.. 1 ..

First-year canes are pale and don't have any side shoots.

Second-year canes will be darker. They will generally have small offshoots coming out of the main stem.

.. 2 ..

.. 3 ..

With autumn-fruiting varieties, cut down all canes after they have fruited. You can be as brutal as you like because only the first-year growth produces fruit. This will help it regenerate the following season with new, fruit-bearing canes. Make sure to wear gloves.

Summer varieties have fruit on second-year growth. After fruiting, cut out all canes that fruited and keep 2–5 of your strongest first-year canes – depending on how big you want the raspberry bush to grow.

.. 4 ..

RASPBERRY

ONE
MINUTE
SKILLS

TRANSPLANTING
STRAWBERRY RUNNERS

Snip and sow – it's that simple

As part of the reproductive cycle most plants will throw out some form of seed, either as part of a seed head, a stand-alone seed or within the flesh of the fruit.

Then there are those that produce magical bonus seedlings that grow out from the plant. In human terms, it would be like starting a family with 3-month-olds who are instantly more developed, less needy and more interesting right from the beginning. Strawberries fit into this category.

There are other plants that also believe in advanced reproduction. The artichoke, for example, will produce mini copies of itself that grow from the main stem of the plant.

1 Strawberry runners shooting off into the distance, trying to find a home.

2 Time to cut the umbilical cord and give them independence. Cut a few millimetres either side of the little seedling using sharp scissors.

3 Free seedling!

4 This part is so straightforward – just like planting any seedling. Pop it where you choose and make sure to water in well. Keep watering it and in no time this guy will be up and running.

ONE MINUTE SKILLS

Zapping snails with copper tape **104**

Netting made easy **106**

Blossom end rot? Don't panic! **110**

Stink-bombing possums **112**

Caterpillars begone! **116**

Coffee-spray your snails away **118**

Keep it clean **120**

What is a soapy spray? **122**

Trapping snails with beer **124**

TOP 5 ⟶ EDIBLE FLOWERS **114**

SHOO, pest!

ZAPPING SNAILS WITH COPPER TAPE

So simple, so effective

Anyone who has ever had a tree get in the way of a breathtaking view or pending development approval will know the consequence of a copper coin – come on, we're all aware of this nasty poisoning tactic! But did you know that copper can be used to kill other stuff too, like pesky snails and slugs?

The copper zaps the skin of the mollusc to disrupt the normal functioning of cells and enzymes. It will usually die within days.

Copper tape around your garden bed or individual plants is a good physical barrier because slugs and snails travel slowly over the tape, giving it enough time to work.

That's not to say that copper tape is the only answer (read through this chapter for more), but it makes up part of the cumulative effort to keep snails and slugs out of the patch.

1 Start by cutting the base off the plastic pot. Remember plastic is usually tough and sharp knives sharp so take care here.

2 Wrap the copper tape around the upper neck of the plastic pot.

3 Place it over the plant you want to protect. When the snail or slug climbs over the copper, it's pretty much goodnight …

4 Rather than doing individual pots you can copper tape entire patches. We often tape our crates and raised garden beds.

ONE
MINUTE
SKILLS

NETTING MADE EASY

Our foolproof guide to keeping the big critters out

We have so much opposition in the patch that sometimes we need to make big moves, and when it comes to the big beasts of the pest world – possums and birds – the only true protection is a net. People are sometimes reluctant to erect netting because of the way it looks. Within seconds poorly erected netting can destroy the look of your garden and every time you look at it you cringe. Yep, vanity in the garden is not lost!

Rather than just throwing a net over the patch and getting yourself in a tangle, there is a straightforward method that makes it easy to install, looks good and will make you feel handy in the process.

2 Start by screwing in the brackets to the outer timber. The length of your screws will depend on your timber – you don't want sharp ends to pop through. If the screws are a little bit too long, screw them in at an angle.

1 The handy hardware: drill, screws, 25 mm brackets, 20 mm electrical conduit (2 x 4 m) and a 4 x 4 m bird net.

3 Simply affix four brackets to opposite sides of the crate. That means eight altogether – two on the top, two on the bottom of each side.

4 To create a sturdy and lightweight frame we use two lengths of 4 m electrical conduit and slot them through the brackets on one side first.

⟫⟫⟫ CONTINUED OVERLEAF

ONE
MINUTE
SKILLS

SHOO, PEST!

108

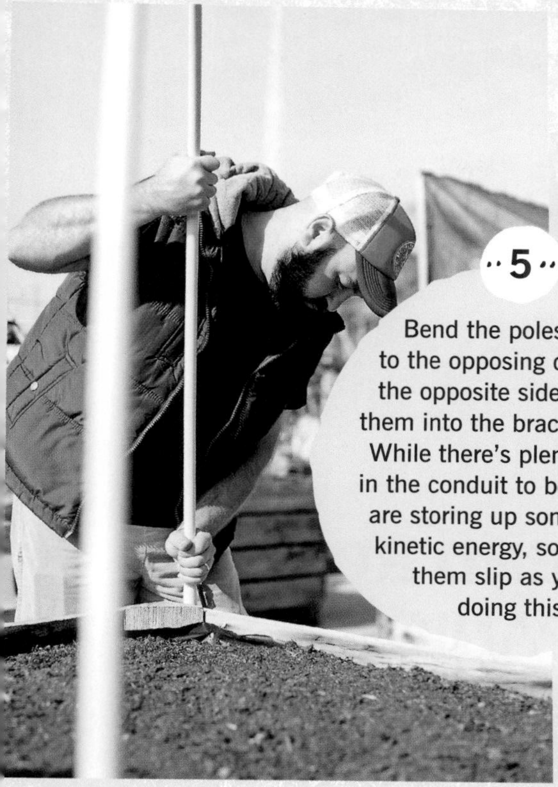

5

Bend the poles down to the opposing corner on the opposite side, slotting them into the brackets there. While there's plenty of give in the conduit to bend it, you are storing up some decent kinetic energy, so don't let them slip as you're doing this.

6

Now throw a net over the top. This is a serious job, so no time for smiles.

8

Hey, good looking!

7

Secure the netting a panel down from the top of your raised bed. Partially insert four screws on each side of the bed (16 in total) to attach the netting. The netting should be taut. Possums like to sit on loose netting and eat the produce through it.

ONE MINUTE SKILLS

BLOSSOM END ROT?
DON'T PANIC!

Just take a deep breath and keep reading ...

Inexperienced and experienced gardeners alike shudder at the sight of blossom end rot – a fungal disease that targets predominantly tomatoes and capsicum. It seems so unnecessary and simply illogical that a perfectly formed, handsome fruit will just start to rot, right there, on the vine.

Newcomers will search for the cause – inconsistent watering and/or insufficient calcium – and quickly try to make amends. Beware: rash action now could prolong the problem.

Don't panic, blossom end rot is a common early-season syndrome! Early spring weather is erratic, at best, and in most cases inconsistent watering has nothing to do with the gardener. Similarly, the gardener is not at fault for calcium deficiency – it's often a trace element plants struggle to take up early on in the piece.

You need to focus on what you can control, and that is keeping your cool.

··1·· Erratic spring weather aside, if you still suspect under-watering your plants is the cause, just ensure they're getting their necessary fix.

··2·· Mulch will help the soil retain a consistent level of moisture. It's the dry, wet, dry, wet thing that is the crux of the problem.

··3·· If the issue persists, additives such as crab shells, eggshells and oyster shells can help lift the calcium uptake of your plants.

··4·· In most cases the problem mends itself and in no time you'll be enjoying the vine-ripened tomatoes you've been dreaming of!

ONE
MINUTE
SKILLS

STINK-BOMBING POSSUMS

Don't get mad, get even

As long as there have been gardens there have been pests, and the possum is about as pesty as they get. Not only do their opposable thumbs make them very capable thieves, but they also easily adapt to deterrents set in their path.

Take a look down the pest control aisle in the hardware store and you will find a suite of products ranging from chilli sprays to high-frequency audio devices – all claiming to be the definitive solution. Unfortunately, possums seem to have developed a fondness for chilli/garlic sprays and those audio devices are much more likely to annoy your poodle than save your lettuce.

As is often the case, the best solution is also the simplest. The only time-tested method to protect a patch is by preventing access to it. Possums are obsessive and habitual creatures who prefer to take the same route into the garden every time. The first line of defence, then, is to disrupt their entry points with barriers. This could be a physical or a 'stink bomb' barrier.

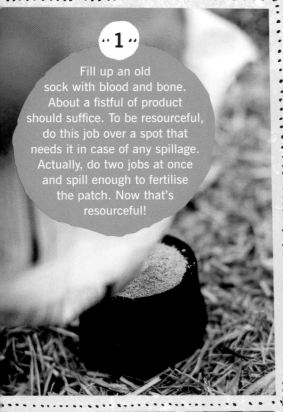

1 Fill up an old sock with blood and bone. About a fistful of product should suffice. To be resourceful, do this job over a spot that needs it in case of any spillage. Actually, do two jobs at once and spill enough to fertilise the patch. Now that's resourceful!

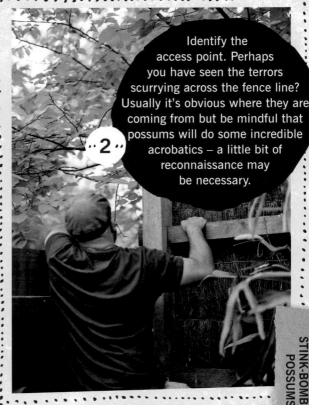

2 Identify the access point. Perhaps you have seen the terrors scurrying across the fence line? Usually it's obvious where they are coming from but be mindful that possums will do some incredible acrobatics – a little bit of reconnaissance may be necessary.

3 Secure the stink bomb somewhere in their immediate path. We used twine to tie it around this fence post.

PUT PLASTIC SPIKES HERE →

4 A stink bomb may not be enough to deter them. It may be worth doubling up with some other preventative measures – such as plastic spikes.

TOP 5 →

Flowers are not only pretty and colourful, they are pretty and colourful *and* can be eaten too. Put these in a bunch (or on your dinner plate) and sweet-talk your way out of any situation.

NASTURTIUM

Pretty, handy and delicious to boot.

The nasturtium comes in many different-coloured varieties and its leaves are edible and delicious too. Add to that its abilities as a pest fighter and pollinator attractor and you've got one hell of a useful plant.

Nasturtiums tend to crowd out plants too closely positioned. Plant 50 cm–1 m apart.

Nasturtiums are best planted in early spring or late autumn.

Nasturtiums are mostly immune to pest and disease issues. Probably the biggest issue is the amount of self-sown seedlings that pop up.

114

NATIVE VIOLA

The native viola is one of the most pretentious flowers around, but it has every right to be.

With its delicate, bright flowers, it's a great pollinator attractor for your other plants.

The native viola is best grown in early spring, giving it time to establish before full summer hits.

The native viola is essentially a groundcover, so don't plant anything much nearby.

Native violas need regular watering when establishing, 3–4 times a week. Once set, cut back to twice a week depending on conditions.

EDIBLE FLOWERS

ROCKMELON

Seriously delicious with goat's cheese wrapped in prosciutto ...

The beauty of any flowering edible plant is that the flavour of its flower is a subtle version of the fruit itself.

Like rockmelon, rockmelon flowers are best planted in spring.

It's a pretty hardy creeper/climber, so don't cramp its style. We like to dedicate a veggie crate purely to rockmelon.

Rockmelon plants produce flowers with ease, but well developed fruit are much more rare. Using them for their flowers means you're guaranteed a result, but it also means sacrificing a shot at the fully developed fruit.

Ugly name, pretty flower.

A flower of lilac that tastes like a cucumber on a castle of thorned leaves. We find pinching the flowers from the plant more satisfying than squeezing a pimple.

Like all flowers, it's best to start growing this early spring.

If you're looking for companion plants, look no further than tomatoes, squash or strawberries.

Not only an excellent companion plant and pollinator attractor, borage adds valuable trace minerals to your soil and makes it more resistant to disease. It is also believed to enhance the flavour of strawberries when planted in close proximity.

BORAGE

Hardy, diverse and versatile. We ♥ chilli.

This is the eyebrow-raiser for your blind taste test as chilli flowers retain elements of the spice contained in the fruit.

Chilli is a heat-loving plant that is best suited to summer growing, but in an appropriately warm space it will continue to produce flowers into winter.

A chilli plant throws out so many flowers and fruit that by sacrificing some of the fruit by eating them as flowers you'll be doing your digestive system a favour.

Much like the fruit itself, chilli flowers range widely in colour and spice.

CHILLI

ONE
MINUTE
SKILLS

CATERPILLARS BEGONE!

When desperate times call for desperate measures

Caterpillar damage in the patch is frustrating. The damage is all too visible while the perpetrators fly invisibly under the radar. Anyone who has taken part in a white cabbage moth caterpillar hunt will know how hard it is to spot the little green guys in the patch, while the holes and poo they leave behind on your broccoli are unavoidable.

Your first line of defence should be fine netting to prevent the moths from landing and laying their eggs, and then using dummy butterflies (see page 172) to disrupt their territorial nature. But if all else fails, then there is a reactive method to control their numbers.

Bacillus thuringiensis, or BT, is a naturally occurring bacteria that can be used to control caterpillar damage in your patch, but it should be considered a last resort. It is not because BT is inorganic, it's just that it is indiscriminate in killing all types of caterpillar species, good and bad. If you do use it, realise that there will be collateral damage.

1 The target: white cabbage moth. They are the nemesis of autumn brassica crops everywhere.

2 You've tried dummy butterflies, you've gone on search-and-destroy missions, and they have even got through your netting: BT is the last-resort remedy.

3 Follow the instructions and dilute the powder in a spray bottle.

4 Spray over the affected crops, making sure it is not a rainy day. Don't do it in the heat of the day either because the sun can cause the foliage to burn. Give it two applications a few days apart.

5 Remember that BT can't discriminate between good and bad, so by using it you're firing bullets at all caterpillar species.

ONE MINUTE SKILLS

COFFEE-SPRAY YOUR SNAILS AWAY

Just in case you need another reason to love coffee

You are either a coffee lover or you are the sort of person who gets wired and nervous at the scent of caffeine. Two guys who go haywire at the thought of coffee are snails and slugs. As if we needed any more reasons to love the stuff.

Coffee to a snail is what red cordial is to a children's birthday party – a really bad idea. The caffeine is something that does not agree with the snail's make-up and one strong hit is enough to poison it.

Although the idea of using perfectly good coffee in the garden does not sit comfortably, in the rare event some is left lying about, this is the next best use for it.

1 An absolute rarity in our house: a partially finished pot of coffee.

2 Dilute 1 part coffee with 5 parts water in a spray bottle – although it will depend on the strength of your brew. The stronger the better – it's the caffeine that's the killer.

3 Spray on and around your affected crops: be liberal. Don't spray in the heat of the day as this may burn the plants. The best time is before nightfall – just before the snails and slugs come out – as this gives the plants time to dry out but the caffeine is still strong.

4 You can also up the ante by using the grounds as an extra line of defence. Fresh coffee grounds are better than used ones but you need to weigh up what's more important …

ONE
MINUTE
SKILLS

KEEP IT CLEAN

A tidy patch is a happy patch

All loved ones need a bit of attention from time to time, and your patch is no different. Being a place where there is so much life, death will also come to pass, either naturally – such as when a plant reaches the end of its life cycle – or prematurely – for example, when you have forgotten to water again or left fruit to rot on the vine.

Unless you're thinking of throwing in the towel and letting the garden go to the dogs, it will need some regular maintenance to keep it hygienic. Weeding, mulching, removing dead and diseased plants, picking produce when ready – this is the usual grooming that is expected.

Just like when cleaning yourself, it's best done routinely, and frequently. Now go and brush your teeth.

The honeymoon phase: everything looking healthy and happy, not a trouble in the world. It's always worth planting more than the space requires but remember to cull as overcrowding will cause you headaches.

1

Perhaps you did nothing much in the first few months and fluked a great-looking patch, but when plants start to produce food, leaving them alone will create troubles. Lettuce and other leafy greens can quickly go to seed, so pull them up to free up space. Remove any rotten fruit as it will attract pests.

2

As plants produce fruit they start to die back – it's a natural occurrence so don't feel like you have done something wrong. Trim back any dead foliage to free up the energy in the plant and reduce the potential for pests and disease.

3

Pick fruit when it's ready: don't let it go to waste!

4

ONE MINUTE SKILLS

WHAT IS A SOAPY SPRAY?

And what do we use it for?

This one is all in the name. A soapy spray is just that – a soap in a spray – and is used to treat sucking pests such as white fly and aphids. If you are unsure if you have a white fly or aphid problem, brush against your plants and if you see a million tiny white or green flies composing a Mexican wave, you have a problem.

The spray works in two ways: firstly by cleaning the plants of any food that the pests may be attracted to and, secondly, by suffocating and killing the critters. It sends out a clear message to the rest of the troublemakers – this is our party and we control the fun.

Although a soapy spray is straightforward, you may have questions you feel are too basic to ask, such as what kind of soap to use, and how soapy should the mixture be? These are very valid questions – thanks for asking.

1 Fill the bottle with water first, then add a good amount of biodegradable washing detergent – enough to clean the dishes from a three-course dinner for four!

2 Do a shake dance. Move it!

3 Spray the affected crops. Don't apply on a rainy day when the spray won't stand a chance of succeeding, or in the heat of the day when the sun can cause the foliage to burn. Like all spray remedies, give it a couple of applications a few days apart.

4 Unless you like the taste of soap on your food it's a good idea to rinse the produce thoroughly before eating.

TRAPPING SNAILS WITH BEER

The sweetest death of all

Beer, poured into a glass, is not just your reward after a tough day on the tools, it is also a sneaky, dirty trap that helps to curb snail numbers in the patch. Those who believe coffee is a wasted commodity used on the veggie patch will be even more vehemently opposed when it comes to using beer. But if you want to protect your crops from pest damage some beer may have to be sacrificed.

You see, snails, like people, are attracted to the smell of yeast, and also find it irresistible. Beer traps placed strategically at their favourite hangout will have that part of the patch abuzz with activity – the queues will be longer than outside the local on a balmy Saturday night!

This is one happy hour too good to be true.

1 Just harvested the beans, mulched the eggplant and composted the wastes. Time for a reward …

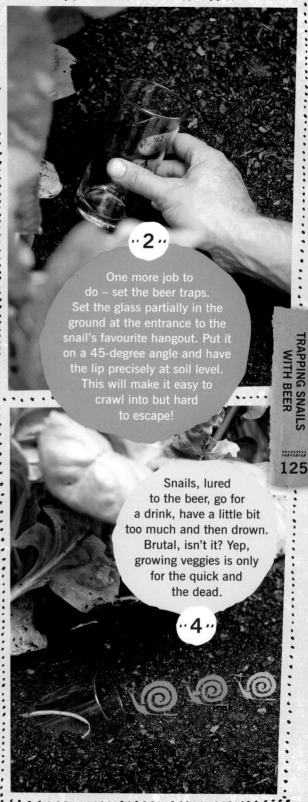

2 One more job to do – set the beer traps. Set the glass partially in the ground at the entrance to the snail's favourite hangout. Put it on a 45-degree angle and have the lip precisely at soil level. This will make it easy to crawl into but hard to escape!

4 Snails, lured to the beer, go for a drink, have a little bit too much and then drown. Brutal, isn't it? Yep, growing veggies is only for the quick and the dead.

3 Pour in the beer – any yeasty product will work just as well – and your trap is set.

ONE
MINUTE
SKILLS

How to harvest herbs **128**

Picking early-season tomatoes **132**

Harvesting leafy greens **134**

Pick more, grow more **138**

How to harvest spring onions **140**

The lowdown on edible flowers **142**

When to pick your beetroot **144**

Root refrigerator **148**

TOP 5 ➤ INVINCIBLES **136**

TOP 5 ➤ TOMATO VARIETIES **146**

GET
picking

ONE
MINUTE
SKILLS

HOW TO
HARVEST HERBS
The essential dos and don'ts

We all have herbs growing in our gardens because of the value they offer, but so often people pick them incorrectly and this affects the return. The biggest mistakes we see are the overenthusiastic haircuts and premature harvests. These are the most detrimental to your herb stocks and leave your patch looking pretty sad. It also reduces your yield.

It's worth noting that not all herbs are made the same and each has its own particular style of harvest. For herbs to love you back they need to be treated like the individuals they are. Rather than taking to them with your finger and thumb, bring in a pair of surgical scissors for maximum precision.

Without question your herbs are important, so slow down and pay attention — this is another opportunity to work on your skills.

2

Not mature enough for picking. You need to let the plant establish for a month or two, depending on weather, before taking your first harvest. Then build on that incrementally – as the plant grows it will provide a larger offering each time you harvest.

1

Someone not trained in the field will take a pair of scissors and cut the bush back down to the stems. Sure, the difference between a bad haircut and a good haircut is two weeks, but some bad haircuts leave you humiliated.

3

Eureka! Herbs ready for picking!

4

With herbs such as basil and sage, cut down to the next junction of new leaves, rather than randomly picking off the leaves that you fancy.

CONTINUED OVERLEAF

ONE
MINUTE
SKILLS

GET PICKING

130

..5..

Parsley is one herb that is picked much like a lettuce. Take from the outer, more mature leaves, leaving the younger growth to become the next generation.

..6..

A lot of herbs, such as oregano, rosemary and thyme, will grow hard and stemmy at the base, while remaining young and tasty on their tops. For these varieties, tip-pruning (harvesting the younger tender tops) is recommended. This encourages the plant to fill out with new growth again.

..7..

A bounty of smartly picked herbs.

..8..

In no time our herbs have replenished their stocks and are ready for more action.

ZINC

ONE
MINUTE
SKILLS

PICKING EARLY-SEASON TOMATOES

Get in quick and minimise the risk

Early spring is one of those beautiful but dangerous times in the veggie patch. The weather is good, prospects are up, but the season also throws in a few erratic punches that can easily knock your plants over. Don't let spring fool you.

Just when you feel on the cusp of the long, bountiful summer, pests and disease come along – concocted by the wild weather – to wreak havoc with your premiere harvest.

There are some things worth gambling with but in our minds early-season tomatoes are not one of those. Too valuable and scarce a commodity, they have been a long time coming – and much anticipated, for that matter – so it would be a shame to let the first taste slip from your grasp.

Sometimes the most cautious approach is the best, and in our minds early-season tomatoes are best picked early. Riper times will just have to wait.

1

Blossom end rot and caterpillar damage are two issues that are prevalent early in the new season. Both are capable of making grown men cry when they infiltrate early-season tomatoes.

2

The damage is more likely to strike as the fruit develops. Unripe green fruit is most unaffected. This is the point when you need to decide on your approach.

3

Sometimes it's best to pick early rather than wait for disaster to strike.

4

The result: not the vine-ripened jackpot, but a healthy dividend. There will be plenty more opportunities to bring the big one home!

ONE
MINUTE
SKILLS

HARVESTING LEAFY GREENS

A handy how-to

Walk through the supermarket and you will most likely come across whole heads of lettuce ready for purchase. If you are lucky you may stumble upon some loose-leaf mix. The supermarkets don't want you to know that this is secretly their cash cow, because all varieties of lettuce (whether hearting or non-hearting), and all leafy greens, in fact, are best harvested leaf by leaf.

To create your own cash cow, harvest the outer, most mature leaves first and work your way in. Freeing up the plant of this old baggage allows it to focus on producing the next generation. Leave enough growth on the plant so it won't feel naked.

This method will reap a perpetual harvest, giving you a truckload more yield than if you pulled the entire head in one fell swoop.

1 Fully developed heads of lettuce are sometimes all that can be found at a supermarket. Later they can be found decomposing in the bottom of your fridge crisper.

2 Ah, the loose-leaf mix – the cash cow!

Now this gives the inner, younger growth a chance to develop. Picking this way gives you the beautiful outcome of a perpetual harvest.

3 Regardless of whether the type of lettuce you're growing is hearting (iceberg, for example) or non-hearting (rocket, for example) all are best picked leaf by leaf. Pick the outer, more mature leaves first.

4

NEW GROWTH!

Green thumb, black thumb, purple thumb, blue thumb ... you don't even *need* thumbs to grow this lot! Neglectful gardeners everywhere, we give you our top five plants that you can't kill ... even if you try.

Yep, Jerusalem artichoke is pretty much immortal.

It is best grown in-ground or in a larger pot.

Unlike the hearting artichoke, the Jerusalem is a tuber – like the potato. It has a very different texture and is much more plentiful.

It's best grown in early spring. Prepare the soil with compost before planting and ensure it is free draining.

Once the plant – a type of sunflower – begins to die back, the tubers are ready to harvest. Use a hand fork or hand trowel to loosen the soil and go digging for treasure.

JERUSALEM ARTICHOKE

Dried, fresh or fried, oregano is delicious.

Oregano is ideally suited to potted growing for balcony gardeners, but it'll appreciate any place you can find for it.

Herbs like oregano grow wild in regions of the Mediterranean, a place where people holiday most of the time and often forget to water. As such is it very hardy.

Oregano grows at any time of the year but will really thrive if given the opportunity to find its feet in spring.

Harvest by tip-pruning, whereby you cut the young growth tips at the top of the plant to encourage it to throw out more.

OREGANO

INVINCIBLES

LEMONGRASS

If you're a fan of Asian food, it is something of a privilege to have lemongrass in your garden.

Lemongrass can be grown in pots but will need a decent-sized vessel to allow for its rigorous root growth. Choose one that is at least 30 cm in depth and diameter.

Being a subtropical plant, it grows best in early spring and goes dormant through winter in temperate climates.

Use plenty of compost when preparing your soil.

To harvest, cut the most mature stems right down at the base of the plant.

Unlike your average geraniums, these smell incredible and are actually worth watering.

Scented geraniums can be grown in pots from 20 cm in depth and diameter upwards.

Scented geraniums boast an amazing range of fragrances. Orange, lime, lemon, apple, mint, apple cider ... we could go on.

These plants are hardy as hell. The stems hold a lot of moisture and the foliage is tough. They don't get burnt very easily and will get by on very little.

To harvest, cut segments of leaves. Rough up the fresh leaves to infuse cold drinks, otherwise dry them for the most flavoursome teas.

SCENTED GERANIUM

ONION

Spend the entire winter away, onions couldn't care less.

Onions are suited to larger pots, but prefer an in-ground veggie patch.

Your soil should be well-drained and low in nitrogen. Onions need lots of potassium, so apply wood ash or potash prior to planting.

Fully bulbing varieties grow best in autumn.

It can take 4–6 months before they're ready for harvest, so kick back and relax. Once the foliage begins to brown and die off, your onions are ready to be harvested.

ONE
MINUTE
SKILLS

PICK MORE, GROW MORE

Harvesting regularly encourages more growth by freeing up the plant for more production.

Leaving food on the plant and admiring it well past its best is not a habit we recommend. Pick often and you will eat often.

The key idea is that any plant can only support a certain amount of fruit at one time. Allowing pods to grow old and haggard will use valuable energy that could be redirected to new growth. It may also bring about other problems, such as rotting fruit on the vine, which will invite pests and disease to the party.

This theory applies to all plants, whether they be beans, peas, tomatoes, zucchini, capsicum ... the food is there for you to eat and if you don't eat it, you will be punished.

1 A bush can quickly become laden with produce and hold no more. It's easy to reach a stalemate where we are not picking any fruit so the plant is not producing any.

2 Pick regularly to free the energy of the plant for more production ... and to have something to eat.

3 Harvesting encourages new flower and pod development, which wouldn't otherwise happen in a full house.

4 Everyone's a winner. You have a bounty of produce and the plant is off doing its business again. So much better than a game of chess.

HOW TO HARVEST SPRING ONIONS

Be smart and reap the rewards

Edible gardening is as much about finesse and skill as it is about diligence and work ethic. Application only gets you so far, but talent can go the distance. So for any precocious talents out there, who happen to be lazy and poorly applied, harvesting spring onions is for you.

Spring onions are the perfect example of a vegetable that can offer more than just one hit. With strong root systems and a constitution that is unfazed by rough handling, it has the ability to be harvested in a 'cut and regenerate' fashion. It also offers more value to the skilled small-space gardener.

Some nice spring onion specimens ready to be harvested.

1

This is the most common way people pick them, ripping out the entire plant and leaving the patch empty.

2

Rather than pulling out the plant, cut the spring onions down near the base – about 1 cm from the ground. This leaves the hearty root system in-ground, still working hard for your patch.

3

In no time the spring onions begin to regenerate and will be ready for another harvest in a few more weeks. By using this technique you are able to get many 'flushes' of harvest rather than one.

4

ONE MINUTE SKILLS

THE LOWDOWN ON EDIBLE FLOWERS

Fine dining meets home cookin'

Flowers can be so much more than just pretty in your garden. They can bring in a plethora of beneficial insects and pollinators to help your patch, they can help keep pests and disease at bay, and they can be cut, arranged and stuck in a vase. Yep, flowers are pretty cool.

Most of us know that flowers can also be eaten, but it is not just the standard few you may have heard about. In fact, every edible plant that produces a flower is producing a form of food that you may not have otherwise considered eating. Every flower out there deserves its time on a plate.

Blind flower taste test anyone?

ONE MINUTE SKILLS

WHEN TO PICK YOUR BEETROOT

In which we apply the 'Goldilocks Principle'

The trick with beetroot is knowing when to eat it – that is, when it's at its absolute best – and that brings us to the 'Goldilocks Principle'. The 'Goldilocks Principle' is a classic gardening theory used for ambiguous advice. Beetroots are 'just right' when they are somewhere between too big and too small. Ha! Just like a bowl of porridge.

We suggest no smaller than a 50-cent piece and no larger than your fist. Or perhaps somewhere between a golf ball and a tennis ball. Anything bigger and it starts to taste like a piece of wood.

The other trick is not being afraid to explore your patch. Root veggies are predominantly anchored at the very base, so they don't mind a bit of scratching around. Pull some mulch and soil away and get a good look at what is growing underneath the surface.

1 A patch full of beetroots – which one is just right? The best way for Goldilocks to find out is to scratch around and see what is happening below the surface.

2 Just because the plant is shooting up a bounty of greens doesn't mean that the root is fully formed. Plants throwing up plenty of green and little root have too much nitrogen in the soil. An application of potassium is necessary in these cases.

3 The opposite is also true. Under a little bundle of foliage may lie a giant's fist of a root! In these cases there is the opposite imbalance of nitrogen and potassium.

4 Just like Goldilocks, if you are going to know what is 'just right', you will have to look at a few. As we said, somewhere between a 50-cent piece and your fist.

TOP 5 →

All the big names and hotshots of the tomato world are here. This is not just about reputation, it's about performance and delivering, year in, year out, to become one of the finest varieties around.

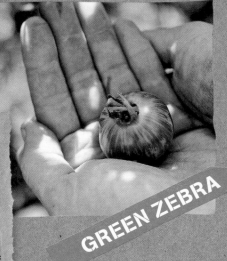

GREEN ZEBRA

A green tomato with racing stripes? All signs say plant!

The Green Zebra's skin is striped and green even when ripe. Wait for the stripes to change from dark to light as the fruit matures. When ready the stripes will be almost orange, but the true ripeness test is in the squeeze – supple with plenty of give.

It's not a huge climber but will need a sturdy 1 m trellis with protection from the afternoon sun. Look to plant in November.

The taste? Very sweet with some bitterness and best suited to salads.

BLACK RUSSIAN

The delectable dark horse of the tomato world.

A ripe Black Russian is incredibly sweet and sugary, but almost meaty too. The flesh is dark, nearing purple, while the outside is more a charcoal infused with red and green.

Like the Green Zebra, this tomato is more about performance than size. You'll need a moderate trellis, no more than 1–1.2 m tall and, because of the sensitivity of the fruit, it will demand shade from the fierce western sun.

You won't get a huge yield so it's all about preserving the numbers that come your way. Fruit is sensitive and can split when left too long on the vine, but at the same time all the flavour is generated through vine ripening.

TOMATO VARIETIES

TOMMY TOE

Failsafe, foolproof ... we love the Tommy Toe.

Tommy Toe is the most honest performer we know. We grow them every year and without fail they come through with the goods. Plant early October.

Two plants will provide enough for a small family. It's a vigorous climber so make sure your trellising system is tall and strong with enough arms to branch out.

Tommy Toes are space greedy and will bully your other spring crops. Make sure to get your spacing right.

For your saucing needs, look no further than the Roma.

An honest Italian – in the same mould as the 1950s immigrants who came to Australia to work in the mines.

Plant for production. Neatly organised rows and columns – if you have the space – with strong trellises to hold the large bundles of fruit they produce. Plant late October to early November.

This is *the* saucing tomato. There are no challengers; the Roma has won all the titles and holds all the belts. The secret is in the pulp yield – a Roma will give you 80% plus, compared with others that struggle to pass 60%.

Romas can get floury with inconsistent watering, so where possible use a drip irrigation system or make sure you're diligent with your watering habits.

ROMA

Good things come in small packages.

We wouldn't blame you for thinking this sultana-sized tomato might swell a bit before ripening. Nope, that's the Tiny Tim: a miniature tomato with a mini taste explosion.

It's quite a small bush, therefore perfect for pots, hanging baskets and wall gardens. Plant in early October.

There's not a hell of a lot to these, so they're best used as a garnish or for presentation.

As the name suggests, this plant stays small. For those who like eating large quantities of food, a Tiny Tim isn't going to satisfy your hunger.

TINY TIM

ONE MINUTE SKILLS

ROOT REFRIGERATOR

Leave what you don't need in the ground

When collecting from the garden it's hard not to let the excitement of the harvest go to your head so that, more often than not, you collect more than necessary. Don't harvest a week's worth of beetroot dinners when all you need is one. Sometimes the smartest harvest is no harvest at all.

All vegetables store differently once picked: some well, others poorly. Of the poor performers, root vegetables are the poorest because once picked they quickly turn limp, soft and spongy – like an inflatable pool horse left out in the hot summer sun.

Rather than getting overexcited, learn how to moderate your picking. Then start to think of your soil as a root refrigerator – somewhere that all root vegetables like to be stored. The efficiency of your root refrigerator will depend on the settings, and these are determined by the seasons.

1

Another overly zealous harvest — way more beetroots and carrots than necessary.

2

The surplus roots quickly turn soft. In this state you will get more enjoyment throwing them at a sibling than you will eating them.

The best setting is during the cooler months of the season, when it is dry. In those conditions the soil will preserve your roots better than Ötzi the iceman.

4

3

Leave ready roots in the soil refrigerator. This is the place they store best, but how well will depend on the settings.

5

As the heat or wet weather intensifies, your refrigerator loses its power and roots are more likely to spoil if left in-ground for too long.

ONE
MINUTE
SKILLS

Drying herbs **152**

Making compost like dough **154**

How to prune a chilli plant **156**

Quick guide to trench-composting **158**

Pickling vegetables **162**

Fermenting waste systems **166**

What worms really love **168**

TOP 5 ⟶ LEAFY GREENS **160**

AFTER the HARVEST

ONE
MINUTE
SKILLS

DRYING HERBS

Maximise your garden bounty

One bad margherita pizza with stale dried oregano is enough to turn you off both margherita pizza and dried oregano. Stale dried herbs have caused so many bad food experiences around the globe we can't blame you for turning away from them.

We're not saying that dried herbs will ever come close to the fresh version, but if oregano is freshly dried and used over a period no longer than 12 months, it will taste much more like oregano on your next margherita pizza and much less like dried cardboard treated with an oregano-scented toilet spray.

Good gardening is all about resourcefulness. Although today there may be mountains of fresh herbs to choose from, there will come a time when they are scarce, so we need to be prepared for best dealing with those scarcities.

2

Hang in a dry, cool place.

1

Pick a bundle, stems and all, and tie together around the base of the stems.

Use your hands to break up the leaves into small flakes. Squeeze, rub, press – whatever works best. Transfer to a jar for storage and date it. Keep for no longer than 12 months and make this an annual exercise.

4

3

Your herbs may be ready in 2–3 weeks. Instead of setting a timer and waiting for it to go off, check after a week or so and track their progress. When they go 'crunch' – like the noise of stepping on dried leaves – they are ready.

OREGANO 2/4/14

ONE MINUTE SKILLS

MAKING COMPOST LIKE DOUGH

That's right: another cooking analogy

Compost is something we can all create at home and it takes only our waste by-products to make. Consider all the kitchen, garden and office waste we throw out daily – nearly all of it is potential compost material. But when you get the balance wrong, the by-product will resemble a stinky pile of garbage rather than a veggie patch commodity.

Just as our cooking skills vary, the ability to make compost does too. Making compost and making bread aren't too dissimilar. Too much water and the dough becomes sticky. Too much flour and it's too dry. Here's how to get it just right.

1 The best way to test your compost is to feel it. If it feels dry, nothing is happening. If it's too wet it'll feel like sludge and stink like garbage – this is because there is no air in it to breathe and an anaerobic process is taking hold.

2 If the compost is too wet you need to add more brown waste. These are things such as cardboard, paper and straw.

3 If the compost is too dry you need to add more moisture – or green waste – such as grass clippings or food scraps.

4 When you are happy with the consistency, it's time to put it to the side and let it bake.

ONE
MINUTE
SKILLS

HOW TO PRUNE
A CHILLI PLANT

And reap the rewards

Chilli plants by nature aren't geared up for hibernation, but that's not to say they can't do it. Surely if a living, breathing creature the size of a bear can sleep in a hole for 6 months and come out the other side alive, so can a plant.

Although technically classified an annual, in more temperate climates you can cut a chilli plant back to a bare skeleton, leaving it dormant for the colder months. Doing this puts the plant in shut-down mode, which is how it remains until the first warm rays of spring sunshine hit its frame. At that point regeneration is imminent and the plant will be active again soon.

When you have identified a great-performing chilli worth keeping, pruning it will help you develop the plant so that it improves through the seasons.

1 As the cool weather intensifies, a chilli plant will start its decline and that is the time to get pruning.

2 Prune right back, leaving the main stem and two or three strong branches. Don't feel like you're hurting the plant – you really want to cut back quite hard, because losing this baggage will help it survive the winter.

3 Some like to pinch back all the leaf growth now as well, but keeping some leaves won't hurt the plant and it helps us to feel good about the garden.

4 As soon as the warm weather returns and the soil heats up sufficiently, the chilli plant sprouts back, bigger, better and stronger than ever.

NEW GROWTH!

ONE MINUTE SKILLS

QUICK GUIDE TO TRENCH-COMPOSTING

When you are short on space, never fear ... Trench-composting is here!

Long before we bought large plastic bins at $80 each to do the composting, our grandparents used to do a thing called trench-composting. As the name suggests, it involves digging trenches in the patch itself as a place to put your food scraps. It is an old-school method Nonno and Nonna used to introduce friendly organisms into the garden and help deal with their wastes.

Back in their day, gardens were much larger and they presented more opportunities to trench-compost. Now, with much smaller spaces at our disposal, rather than leaving land idle in order to trench-compost, use this method to deal with excess scraps when the opportunity presents itself.

Trench-composting aside, a compost bin, worm farm and/or fermenting waste system should still be part of your recycling system.

Find some vacant real estate and dig your trench line — it should be at least 30 cm deep and a similar width. A small kid's shovel is well suited to this job.

1

2

Tip in your compost scraps. The depth of the trench will help to create heat for the microbes to come and decompose the scraps. Worms will do part of the job for you and produce castings too.

A month or two down the track and the scraps have been converted into chocolatey, rich compost.

3

Cover over, firm down and wait. This is the easiest form of composting because it requires no maintenance. The compost is 'baking' directly in the garden, exactly where you need it.

4

TOP 5 →

There is much confusion in the world of leafy greens. to the untrained palate lettuces can be misinterpreted as simply piles of green leaves. It's time to focus on the best rabbit food around and issue the definitive guide.

Best-in-show salad? Crispy pigs' ear salad with mustard greens and apple.

- This is hot English mustard in leaf form – it's bitey and strong. You only need a little bit in a dish to infuse the food with its flavour, so it gives great value in the kitchen.
- **It'll take off equally well in autumn or spring, but then hit different hurdles as the season shifts. Summer will make it very hot – like wasabi – and push it to seed, while winter makes it susceptible to pests.**
- You'll get a harvest in about the same length of time it takes to recover from eating wasabi through your nose – about 4 weeks.

MUSTARD GREENS

Best-in-show salad? Team with balsamic syrup and pecorino.

- Bitey and peppery, rocket is a must in any self-respecting Italian's patch. Its flavour intensifies with age.
- **Rocket grows best in cool conditions. If the plant starts to go to seed, pick off the seed heads as they appear (see page 72). This should transfer growth back to the leaf.**
- Rocket is susceptible to the white cabbage moth in cooler months, so do your best to prevent their impact (see pages 116 and 172).
- **Pick leaf by leaf from four weeks after germination onwards.**

ROCKET

LEAFY GREENS

MIZUNA

Best-in-show salad? Mizuna with walnuts, goat's cheese, sultanas and balsamic-pickled shallots.

- Mizuna is quite watery with only a mild, sweet bitterness – it's the appearance of the leaf that is eye-catching and it gives a nice aesthetic to your salads.

- **It is best grown in the middle of spring and autumn, but, like all leafy greens, it is not particularly fussed.**

- In seedling form, mizuna generally comes in a tight square punnet that demands some fiddly separation (see how on page 51).

Best-in-show salad? Anything with French components. French sorrel with French shallots soaked in French sherry.

- Very similar to sorrel, except French, so it sounds exotic and this makes it more attractive. Also gives it a little more flair on the dinner plate.

- **Plant French sorrel in early autumn or early spring.**

- French sorrel can get quite bitter when it goes to seed or is grown in the heat of summer. Much like its Anglo counterpart, leave it too long in the ground and it'll begin to taste like lemon rind.

- **It won't let you touch it until it is more than ready, which is usually about 4–6 weeks into your relationship.**

FRENCH SORREL

Best-in-show salad? One that features silverbeet in small quantities and uses only the youngest leaves.

- Silverbeet is the champion of leafy greens – lauded for its consistency and no-fuss attitude. While never a standout, it is always the first name on the team sheet.

- **Plant it anytime, anywhere. Okay, perhaps not that loosely; remember it is still a plant and does have some needs – albeit quite basic ones.**

- Silverbeet can go to seed when you're sick of the sight of it and can't bring yourself to pick another leaf.

- **Silverbeet is a grazing green – simply snap off the outer leaves as you need them. This is usually 6 weeks in.**

SILVERBEET

PICKLING VEGETABLES
Nonna's secrets revealed

Pickling is a great way of infusing old tastes with new flavours. It also greatly increases the shelf life of your produce. One of the skills of a seasonal eater is making sure bountiful seasons can be revisited when things get bleak — and pickling stinks of good times.

Wrapping your head around the pickling process can sometimes prove troublesome because recipes and theories are as varied as the colour of the underpants you wear. Some picklers prefer sitting their produce in brine, while others favour the sharpness of vinegar. There are no right or wrong ways to pickle and none are difficult, but the many different ways do make it seem complex.

We think it is about time to provide some clarity: our favourite recipe is Nonna's 3:2:1. We're going to use beetroot here, but you can use almost any vegetable.

1 Like making bread, pickling isn't nearly as difficult as you expect it to be. Start by bathing the glass jars in some boiling water and then set them aside to cool.

2 Give the beetroots a rinse and chop off the tops and bottoms – bigger ones can be cut in half to help them cook more evenly.

3 Boil the beetroots until a knife slides in easily but then meets some resistance towards the centre. Once done the skins will rub off easily under running water; this saves some hassle and mess later on.

4 The thinner the slices the faster the pickle mixture will work its magic. The thickness of slices also affects the texture, so cut according to your preference.

CONTINUED OVERLEAF

2

↓

VINEGAR

3

↓

WATER

1

↓

SUGAR

..6..

Prepare the sterilised jars by adding some spices. For a 500 ml jar we add a teaspoon of coriander seeds, a teaspoon of mustard seeds, five cloves and a couple of pieces of lemon rind.

..5..

Depending on the number of jars and veggies, the quantity of your pickling mixture will vary. All you need to do is ensure you combine water, vinegar and sugar to the magic ratio 3:2:1 (plus a pinch of salt) and bring to the boil.

..8..

Best to wait about 3 weeks, depending on the thickness of the beetroot. Beyond that, these little treats should last just about as long as Nonna has.

..7..

From here, simply pack in the beetroot and fill the jar with the warm mixture so that everything is covered. Fill as closely to the top as you dare to ensure the jar becomes airless as it cools (and therefore airtight).

ONE MINUTE SKILLS

FERMENTING WASTE SYSTEMS

What are they and how do we use 'em?

Having used many apple orchard fruit bins as veggie gardens over the years, we've come across a lot of fermenting apples. From our experience, fermentation is not particularly pleasant – it smells precisely like rotten apples. But speak to wine, beer and cider makers and they would strongly disagree – they know that fermentation is essential to create their drinks of choice.

In the same way, fermenting waste systems are a great way of creating the drink of choice for your veggie patch. They are also the most compact system available and perfectly suited to inner-city gardening.

Whenever you put waste into your system, apply the fermentation accelerator. Some are powders, others are sprays. Use more after adding high-protein foods such as meat, fish, eggs and cheese. Because this is an anaerobic process, it requires no air, and the lid needs to be closed at all times!

1

Check for juice often and use it on the garden. The juice is full of nutrition from the food scraps and is alive with micro-organisms! The juice should be diluted 1 teaspoon for every 2 L of water.

2

Once the bin is full, bury the waste in the same way as trench-composting – just mix in some soil before adding it to the trench and burying. It makes the soil acidic, so wait a few weeks before planting young seedlings into it.

3

Make sure to wash the bin after each use and then it's time to get fermenting again!

4

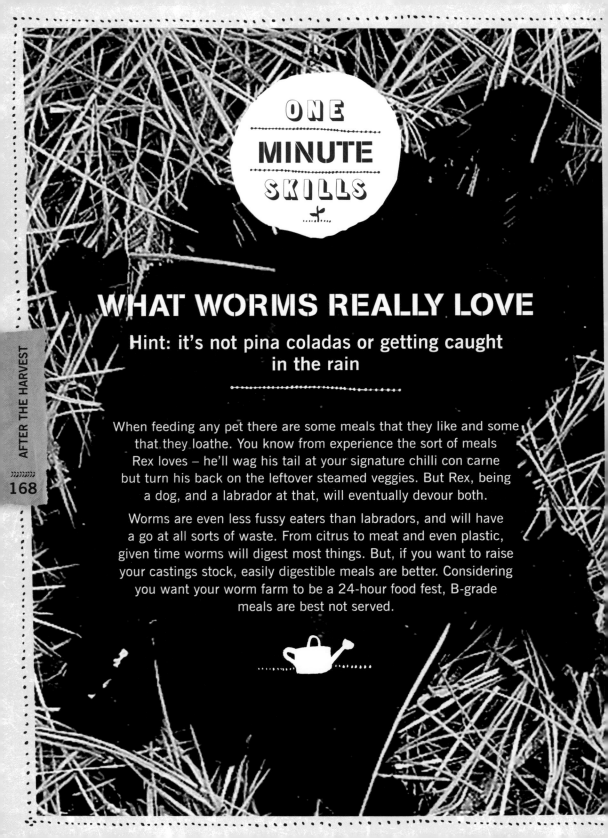

ONE MINUTE SKILLS

WHAT WORMS REALLY LOVE

Hint: it's not pina coladas or getting caught in the rain

When feeding any pet there are some meals that they like and some that they loathe. You know from experience the sort of meals Rex loves – he'll wag his tail at your signature chilli con carne but turn his back on the leftover steamed veggies. But Rex, being a dog, and a labrador at that, will eventually devour both.

Worms are even less fussy eaters than labradors, and will have a go at all sorts of waste. From citrus to meat and even plastic, given time worms will digest most things. But, if you want to raise your castings stock, easily digestible meals are better. Considering you want your worm farm to be a 24-hour food fest, B-grade meals are best not served.

1

Worms that feed well will produce more baby worms, which will also need proper feeding. More worms, more feeding, more castings.

2

Your worms love: coffee grounds, eggshells, tea bags, paper products and veggie/fruit scraps.

Your worms don't like: citrus, the onion family, dairy, meat products and Rex's poo.

3

4

Feed your worms what they love and they will feed you!

ONE
MINUTE
SKILLS

Making dummy butterflies **172**
Making egg-carton planters **176**
Seed-bombing **178**
Competitive snail-hunting **182**
Decorating the patch **184**

TOP 5 ➝ FAST-GROWERS **174**

LITTLE

helpers

MAKING DUMMY BUTTERFLIES

**Keep your friends close, but your enemies closer.
The same applies in the veggie patch and it's
worth knowing your pests intimately.**

Of all the pests in the garden the white cabbage moth is one of our primary nemeses, and funnily enough it is often confused for and admired as a pretty white butterfly roaming the garden. Oh, the irony!

It is not the moth itself that is doing the damage but the moth larvae. These camouflaged green caterpillars have huge appetites for your sweet brassica crops and leafy greens. A happy patch can quickly turn ugly – full of these mini monsters spoiling your hard-earned crops.

One avenue is the physical barrier – setting up fine netting over your garden – but another preventative measure, and one that allows you to get your craft on and involve the kids, is making dummy butterflies. Thankfully, while the white cabbage moth larvae are incredibly destructive with huge appetites, the moths are territorial, mostly blind and a little stupid, so bits of plastic dangling on wires can be enough to keep them at bay.

1

Our crafting tools: plastic shopping bag, thin wire, thick wire, scissors and tin snips.

2

Cut the plastic bag into 10 cm x 5 cm strips. Pinch the middle of each strip and secure with the thin wire to create the butterfly bodies.

Get the kids to help you place them around the patch where the larvae have been causing trouble.

4

Trim the wings to make them round. Cut 40–50 cm lengths of the thicker wire and attach the butterflies to them.

3

TOP 5 ⟶

These veggies are the ones best suited to people with short attention spans or who are in need of instant gratification. That may well be your 8-year-old, but, more likely, it's you.

ZUCCHINI

From the second month on, zucchini will be hitting the party scene hard, dragging along the entire ratatouille crew.

- Zucchini is best grown in an in-ground veggie patch. Space plants 1 m apart and grow them in spring.
- **Water 3–4 times a week initially and then cut back to twice a week when mature.**
- Zucchini likes a bit of space to cut loose and needs sunshine. Soil should be free draining, with plenty of compost.
- **Left on the bush too long, zucchini will become aerated and tasteless with tough skin. Pick frequently and dispose of any fruit that doesn't pollinate properly in the compost.**

BUTTERHEAD LETTUCE

Butterhead's calendar is pretty open, so you'll only need to give 2–3 weeks' notice for a dinner party.

- Butterhead is suited to smaller pots – 10 cm in depth will be fine. Space plants 20 cm apart.
- **Butterhead grows well all year round but does best in spring. It needs soil with adequate nitrogen – compost will do – and regular watering, but otherwise ain't fussy.**
- Butterhead will keep on giving just as long as you keep on taking. Perpetually harvest leaf by leaf, taking from the outer more mature leaves and working your way in.

FAST-GROWERS

Spring onion only takes a month or so to get dressed and ready.

- Suited to smaller pots – 15 cm in depth will suffice. Space plants 2–5 cm apart. Spring onion plants don't mind being packed in together, so they're good space-savers.

- **Plant in a fertile, friable soil. While spring onion plants can tolerate shade, they'll grow faster with plentiful sun.**

- Water in daily when establishing then cut back to 2–3 times a week. Apply liquid fertiliser every fortnight.

SPRING ONION

Our favourite variety is Cherry Belle – named after the Indonesian girl band.

- Radishes are suited to smaller pots, 10–15 cm in depth. Space plants 2–5 cm apart, depending on the dexterity of your fingers.

- **Radishes like a mix of cool and warm, with even moisture. By that we mean the best of autumn and spring, without all the erratic stuff. Make sure your soil is well drained and not too nitrogen-heavy.**

- Water 2–3 times a week over their lifetime.

- **In cooler, wet weather, radishes become susceptible to snails and slugs, so set up your defence boundaries and launch a pre-emptive strike (see page 104).**

RADISH

Unless you're skilled at converting a chopstick into a cutting tool, you might like to try dwarf bok choi.

- Bok choi is suited to smaller pots. Space plants 20–30 cm apart.

- **It likes moist, fertile soil and requires high levels of nitrogen.**

- Bok choi prefers warmth and humidity, so spring is perfect – however, it can be grown at most times of the year.

- **Pick leaf by leaf, from the outer more mature leaves working inwards. If you decide you want the entire plant, cut it off with a knife a few centimetres from the ground and let the roots reshoot new growth (you can do this 2–3 times).**

BOK CHOI / PAK CHOI

ONE
MINUTE
SKILLS

MAKING EGG-CARTON PLANTERS

An eggscellent rainy day activity

Sometimes you do things to save money, sometimes you do things because you read about them online and sometimes you do things because you have a lot of egg cartons. Egg-carton planters probably won't save you enough money to retire, but it is just one more piece of material not going into the bin.

This is a resource that most people handle every week and probably just toss out with the recycling. The materials that make up the carton are almost identical to the jiffy pots you purchase from a nursery – same size and biodegradable! The tops of cartons work well as seed trays and individual egg holders make great vessels to carry your seedlings into the patch.

Although it sounds a bit too easy to be a 'project', this is a fantastic children's activity and a good way to spend a couple of hours. Put on some good music, break out the craft kit and turn each planter into its own character!

··1··
Jiffy pots: biodegradable seed planters that you can buy from a nursery and use for propagating seeds.

··2··
Egg carton: biodegradable seed planters that you can buy from a market with eggs in them and use for propagating seeds.

It's just a matter of filling up with seed-raising mix (potting mix will work just fine too) and planting your seeds. When the plants are ready for transplanting to the patch, rather than removing the cartons, bury them and they will decompose.

··4··

··3··
There are two useful pieces that come from the one carton: the lid is a great seed tray for propagating smaller stuff such as radish, carrots or beetroot, while the individual cells can be cut apart to make seed cells for larger varieties.

ONE MINUTE SKILLS

SEED-BOMBING
Guerilla gardening, Rambo-style

Seed-bombing is an old guerilla-gardening special, and one that is great fun for the kids. It's a special type of warfare that creates life rather than destroying it. You get to choose which life to create and where you want to create it.

Seed-bombing originated as a way of beautifying derelict and hard-to-get-at land. It's a rapid-fire way of getting things started but the survival rate of the bombs is 50/50. With seed-bombing it's all about the numbers and the timing.

The first part is pretty simple: the more bombs that land on the site, the greater the chance of some propagating and taking hold. When it comes to timing, the closer the attack coincides with a period of wet and warm weather, the greater the survival rate.

That's why we put our best man on this job.

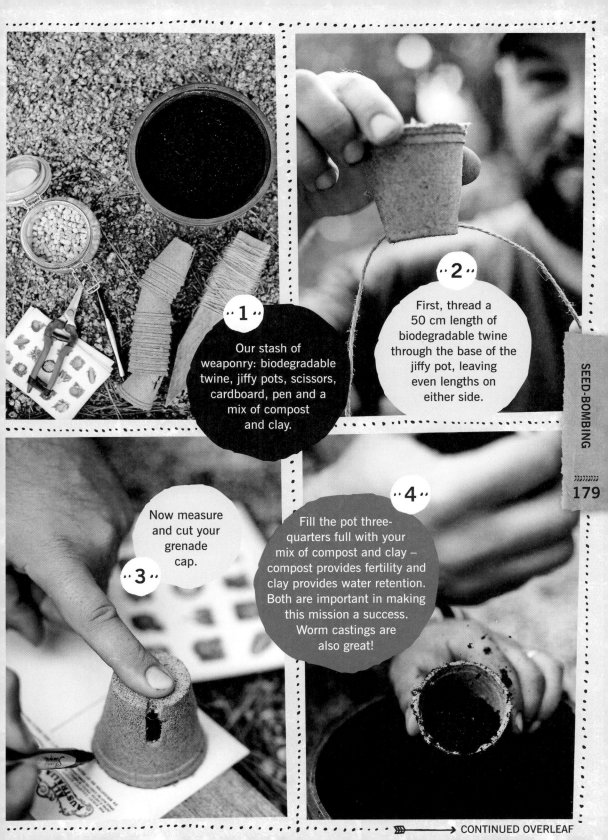

1
Our stash of weaponry: biodegradable twine, jiffy pots, scissors, cardboard, pen and a mix of compost and clay.

2
First, thread a 50 cm length of biodegradable twine through the base of the jiffy pot, leaving even lengths on either side.

3
Now measure and cut your grenade cap.

4
Fill the pot three-quarters full with your mix of compost and clay – compost provides fertility and clay provides water retention. Both are important in making this mission a success. Worm castings are also great!

CONTINUED OVERLEAF

LITTLE HELPERS

180

··5··

Pop in a couple of seeds and cover over with more mix.

Now lid the jiffy and tie it off with the twine.

··6··

··7··

'Attention! Special Corporate Fabian Capomolla reporting for duty, Sir! Yes, Sir!'

We thought the time had passed when we could pretend we're throwing hand grenades over enemy lines. How wrong we were! We have just seed-bombed the hell out of this place!

··8··

ONE MINUTE SKILLS

COMPETITIVE SNAIL-HUNTING
Child labour at its most effective

There is nothing like a pest remedy that produces tangible results you can see and organising an enthusiastic team of young ones to pick the snails out of your veggie patch should fill you with great confidence that something is finally getting done in the garden.

Sometimes there is nothing more satisfying than an old-fashioned search-and-destroy mission.

Going after snails needs to be well timed. Success isn't guaranteed when searching for them on a hot, dry day; instead, target your efforts to when they are more likely to be out: on a cool, damp morning. You can also provide artificial hideouts a couple of days prior. Any object that offers a dark, damp hideout will work.

Aside from curbing pests, organising your children to collect snails will free up time to get other important stuff done, such as the cryptic crossword.

1 Gather a search team and gear them up for the job. Early in the morning is the best time, particularly if it's damp. Look for dark, wet places that have some cover; this is where the snails will be hiding.

2 Set some targets for the collection and don't let the party return without sufficient numbers.

The haul!

3

4 Unfortunately this is not a search and rescue operation, it's search and destroy. Time to take the snails for 'a walk'.

ONE MINUTE SKILLS

DECORATING THE PATCH

Take pride in your patch and it shall flourish

Although it seems nothing more than vanity, decorating your veggie patch will make it a more alluring place for the gardeners and a less enticing one for the pests. By brightening up the colour scheme and bringing in a few new additions you can give energy and a sense of ownership to those who need it most. A patch makeover could be the tonic your garden needs.

It will also give you a family project that you can draft the kids into.

Dust off the craft box and slap on a smock. Gather all your interior design magazines together and start sifting through ideas. It's decorating time and there is no harm in taking it quite seriously.

1 Nothing like a coat of paint to brighten the place up. Sort out your favourite colours to slap on the patch.

2 Add a little more personality with a scarecrow. Even if it doesn't frighten the birds it will hopefully freak out your children's friends and that means less sleepovers.

Give your patch a name, make it a friend.

3

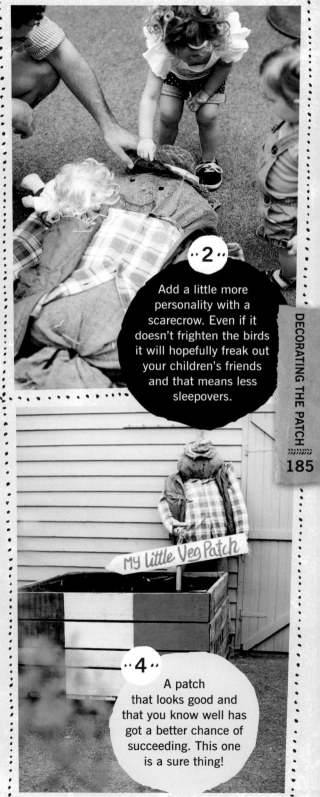

My little Veg Patch

4 A patch that looks good and that you know well has got a better chance of succeeding. This one is a sure thing!

ACKNOWLEDGEMENTS

HERBS

EDIBLE
PLANTS
GIFTS
GARDENING
LANDSCAPE
SERVICES

GROW YOUR OWN
TEA HERBS
LEMON VERBANA
MINT
LEMON BALM
CAMOMILE

A special thanks to our co-worker and friend, Dillon, for inspiring *1-Minute Gardener* and to the gang at Plum for realising it.

Thanks Mary Small for another fun, easy and most enjoyable collaboration and Clare Marshall for all your hard work in seeing this through. You provided beautiful little children when required and we almost got our hands on those purple beans!

So nice to work with John Laurie again, and see the worlds of edible gardening and moody photography collide one more time. Thanks also to Tom Friml for the precise touches and any soil site analysis that was required.

Incredible to finally meet you Miss Mackintosh! This book has really come alive with your lovely design and illustrations. Thanks most of all for making sure we looked awesome on the front cover.

Thanks to Martine Lleonart, our editor, for sifting through the mess of copy and polishing it up so well.

To the Sharpley family for lending us their garden and home. Best of luck on the big move to the Benton Rise Farm and we hope to see you down there soon.

To the Pember family for always letting us use their garden as a test site, and for stocking the fridge whenever we do.

To Emi, Marlowe, Elvie and Nina for being gorgeous, attentive and the perfect little helpers. You're all so advanced!

And finally to all the guys and girls at the Little Veggie Patch Co. for growing with us.

ACKNOWLEDGEMENTS

187

INDEX

A

acidic soil 28–9, 167
alkaline soil 28–9
alliums *see* chives, garlic,
    onions, spring onions
aphids 122
artichokes 100
    see also Jerusalem
        artichoke
asbestos 23

B

Bacillus thuringiensis (BT)
    116, 117
basil 51, 59, 129
beans 56, 65, 138–9
    climbing 59
    soaking seeds 40–1
    see also broad beans
beer traps 124–5
beetroot 59
    harvesting 144–5,
        148–9
    pickling 162–5
    soaking seeds 40–1
beneficial insects 58, 142
berries *see* raspberries,
    strawberries
birds 106
Black Russian tomatoes
    146
blood and bone 21, 113
blossom end rot 110–1,
    133
bok choi 175
borage 115, 143
brassicas 13, 65, 117,
    172

see also broccoli,
    cabbage, cauliflower
broad beans 65
    soaking seeds 40–1
broccoli 65
    flowers 143
butterflies, dummy 172–3
butterhead lettuce 174

C

cabbage 65
cabbage moths *see* white
    cabbage moths
calcium 110, 111, 138
capsicum
    blossom end rot 110–1
    mulching 85
carrots 59
    harvesting 148
caterpillars 116–17, 133,
    172
celery 59
cherry tomatoes *see*
    tomatoes
chillies 115
    flowers 143
    pruning 156–7
chives 51, 59
    flowers 143
citrus trees 87, 89
climbing plants 56–7
climbing spinach 57
coffee grounds 119, 169
coffee spray 118–19
companion planting 58–9
compost 25
    amount to use 26–7
    making 154–5

mushroom compost 31
    trench-composting
        158–9
containers 23
    see also crates, pots
contaminates, testing for
    22–3
copper tape 104–5
coriander 47, 51
corn *see* sweetcorn
crates
    copper taping 105
    lining 18–9
crop rotation 64–5
cucumbers 57
    pinching 91
culling 43, 45, 55,
    74–5, 121

D

deciduous trees 87, 89
dill 51
diseases 68, 121, 132,
    138, 142
    blossom end rot 110–1,
        133
    fungal 71, 110–1
    sooty mould 47, 71
    stem rot 85
    see also pests
dolomite lime 29
drying herbs 152–3
dummy butterflies 172–3

E

easy-growing plants 20–1
edible flowers 114–5,
    142–3

egg-carton planters, making 176–7
eggplants 59
  incubating seedlings 53
  mulching 85
evergreen trees 87

F

fast-growing plants 174–5
fermenting waste systems 166–7
fertilising
  potted plants 80–1
  reducing need for 26–7, 58–9, 64–5
  see also compost
flowers 58
  edible 114–5, 142–3
  foliage, dead 121
French sorrel 161
fruit trees, pruning 86–9
fruit, picking 121
fungal diseases 71, 110–1

G

gall wasps 89
garden beds *see* veggie patch
garlic 47, 59
  planting 60–1
geranium, scented 137
germination 40, 41, 43, 45
Green Zebra tomatoes 146

H

harvesting 138–9
  beetroot 144–5, 148–9
  early-season tomatoes 132–3
  herbs 128–31

leafy greens 134–5
root vegetables 148–9
spring onions 140–1
herbs 58, 76
  annual 76
  drying 152–3
  harvesting 128–31
  perennial 30, 76
  planting seedlings 51
  transplanting 30, 31
  see also basil, chives, coriander, dill, lemon balm, mint, oregano, parsley, rosemary, sage, thyme, Vietnamese mint

I

iceberg lettuce 135
insects, beneficial 58, 142
invincible plants 136–7

J

Jerusalem artichokes 136

L

leafy greens 13, 72, 121, 160–1, 172
  harvesting 134–5
  see also bok choi, French sorrel, lettuce, mustard greens, mizuna, pak choi, rocket, silverbeet, sorrel
leeks 59
lemon balm 47
lemongrass 137
lettuce 59, 65, 72, 76, 121, 134–5, 174
lime, dolomite 29
lucerne hay 25, 31
  see also mulch

M

marigolds 143
melons *see* rockmelon, watermelon
microclimates 37
mint 20
  see also Vietnamese mint
mizuna 161
mulch 25, 31, 111, 120
  applying 82–5
  topping up beds 31
mustard greens 160

N

nasturtium 59, 114, 143
native viola 114
netting 106–9, 116
nitrogen 56, 59, 65, 76, 77, 137, 145, 174, 175
no-dig gardens 19
  topping up 30–1

O

onions 59, 65, 137
oregano 51, 131, 136

P

pak choi 175
parsley 51, 131
pea straw mulch 25, 31, 82–3
  see also mulch
peas 56, 65, 138
  pinching 91
  soaking seeds 40–1
pest control 52, 59, 68, 114, 121, 142
  Bacillus thuringiensis (BT) 116, 117
  beer traps 124–5

INDEX

coffee spray 118–19
competitive snail hunting
182–3
copper tape 104–5
dummy butterflies
172–3
netting 106–9
soapy spray 122–3
stink bombs 112–3
see also pests
pests 69, 121, 132, 138,
160, 172
aphids 122
birds 106
caterpillars 116–17
competitive snail hunting
182–3
gall wasps 89
possums 106, 109,
112–13
snails and slugs 104–5,
118–19, 124–5
sucking 122
white cabbage moth
116–17
white fly 122
see also diseases, pest
control
pH level 25, 28–9
pickling vegetables
162–5
pinching 90–1
planters, egg-carton
176–7
planting
companion planting
58–9
crop rotation 64–5
depths 43
seedlings 38–9, 48–51
seeds 42–5

spacing 54–5
time of day 38–9
time of year 36–7
tomatoes 62–3
plants
climbing 56–7
culling 43, 45, 55,
74–5, 121
easy-growing 20–1
fast-growing 174–5
invincible 136–7
shade-loving 46–7
small-space 76–7
see also planting
pollination 57, 58, 59
hand-pollination 57,
94–7
pollinators 58, 94, 142
pollinator attracting
plants 59, 114, 115
possums 106, 109,
112–13
potash 137
potassium 137, 145
potatoes 77
pots
choosing 14–5
fertilising 80–1
pruning
chilli plants 156–7
fruit trees 86–9
raspberries 98–9
pumpkins 57
hand-pollination 94–5
pinching 91

R

radishes 21, 59, 75, 77,
175
raised garden beds 16–7
copper taping 105

netting 106–9
see also crates
raspberries, pruning 98–9
rocket 73, 135, 160
rockmelon 115
hand-pollination 95
Roma tomatoes 147
root vegetables, harvesting
148–9
rosemary 51, 131
rotten fruit 121, 138
see also blossom end rot

S

sage 51, 129
scarecrows 185
scented geranium 137
seed heads, picking 72–3
seed-bombing 178–81
seedlings
culling 74–5
incubating 52–3
planting 38–9, 48–51
strawberry runners
100–1
tomatoes 63
seeds
picking seed heads
72–3
planting 42–5
soaking 40–1, 43
shade-loving plants 46–7
silverbeet 20, 161
slugs 59, 104–5, 118–19,
175
small-space plants 76–7
snails 104–5, 118–9,
124–5, 175
competitive hunting
182–3
soapy spray 122–3

soil
  acidic 28–9, 167
  additives for calcium 111
  alkaline 28–9
  improving 24–5
  pH level 25, 28–9
  testing for contaminates
    22–3
sooty mould 47, 71
sorrel 47
  French sorrel 161
spinach 59
  climbing 57
spring onions 21, 59, 175
  harvesting 140–1
squash 21
  companion planting 115
  hand-pollination 94–5
stem rot 85
stink-bombing possums
  112–3
strawberries 59, 77
  companion planting 115
  transplanting runners
    100–1
sugar cane mulch 25, 31,
  82–5
  see also mulch
sulphur 29
sunlight 13
  chasing 16–7
  and planting 39
sweetcorn 59
  soaking seeds 40–1

T

thyme 51, 131
Tiny Tim tomatoes 147
tomatoes 59, 65, 138
  blossom end rot 110–1
  companion planting 115

culling seedlings 75
  early-season picking
    132–3
  flowers 143
  mulching 85
  planting times 62–3
  staking 92–3
  varieties 146–7
Tommy Toe tomatoes 147
transplanting
  herbs 31
  seedlings 48–9, 52–3
  strawberry runners
    100–1
  transplant shock 73
trees 13
  pruning fruit trees 86–9
trellising 32–3
trench-composting 158–9

V

veggie patch
  choosing spot for 12–3
  decorating 184–5
  maintaining 120–1
vertical gardens 16–7
Vietnamese mint 46
violas 143
  native viola 114

W

waste systems, fermenting
  166–7
water retention 25
watering 70–1, 110, 111
  amount 70–1, 79
  fan-spray 78–9
  timing 68–9
weeding 120
white cabbage moth
  116–7, 160, 172

white fly 122
wood ash 137
worms 25
  food for 168–9
  worm castings 25, 31,
    159, 168, 169, 179
  worm farms 158, 168–9

Z

zucchini 138, 174
  culling seedlings 75
  hand-pollination 94–7
  identifying male/female
    flowers 96

A Plum book

This amended edition published in 2021 by
Pan Macmillan Australia Pty Limited

First published in 2014 by
Pan Macmillan Australia Pty Limited
Level 25, 1 Market Street,
Sydney, NSW 2000, Australia

Level 3, 112 Wellington Parade,
East Melbourne, Victoria 3002, Australia

Design by Michelle Mackintosh
Typesetting by Megan Ellis
Edited by Martine Lleonart

Index by Helena Holmgren
Photography by John Laurie
Colour reproduction by Splitting Image Colour Studio
Printed and bound in China by Imago Printing
International Limited

A CIP catalogue record for this book is available from
the National Library of Australia.

The publisher would like to thank the Sharpley family
for their generosity in providing one of the locations for
the book.

10 9 8 7 6 5 4 3 2 1